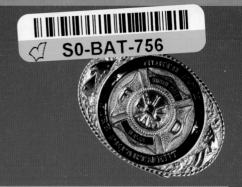

Collecting Men's Belt Buckles

Dr. Joseph V. Saitta

4880 Lower Valley Road, Atglen, PA 19310 USA

Dedication

I'd like to especially thank the members of my family for their understanding and patience as I have collected my way through life. This book is fondly dedicated to them: Pat, Phil, John, Sandie, Chris, Megan, and Joseph. I couldn't have completed this book without their help.

Naturally, special thanks to my wife, Pat, who has borne the greatest burden of living with a man who has the "collecting gene."

Copyright © 2001 by Dr. Joseph V. Saitta
Library of Congress Card Number: 00-109729

Designed by John P. Cheek
Type set in Americana XBd BT/Souvenir Lt BT
ISBN: 0-7643-1296-0
Printed in China
1 2 3 4

Published by Schiffer Publishing Ltd.
4880 Lower Valley Road
Atglen, PA 19310
Phone: (610) 593-1777; Fax: (610) 593-2002
E-mail: Schifferbk@aol.com
Please visit our web site catalog at
www.schifferbooks.com

In Europe, Schiffer books are distributed by
Bushwood Books
6 Marksbury Ave.
Kew Gardens
Surrey TW9 4JF England
Phone: 44 (0)20-8392-8585
Fax: 44 (0)20-8392-9876
E-mail: Bushwd@aol.com
Free postage in the UK. Europe: air mail at cost

This book may be purchased from the publisher.
Include $3.95 for shipping.
Please try your bookstore first.
We are always looking for people to write books on new and related subjects. If you have an idea for a book please contact us at the above address.
You may write for a free catalog.

Contents

Acknowledgments 4
Introduction 5
Public Safety Buckles 12
Military Buckles 58
Youth Group Buckles 107
Western Style Buckles 117
Multi-function Buckles 126
Future Collecting Categories 133
Resources 158

Corrections and Future Editions

Although a great deal of care has been taken in researching this book, errors will no doubt be present. The identification of foreign buckles, in particular, has been difficult. If you notice any errors, please contact me so that I may correct them in future editions. Also, I'd like to hear your comments and suggestions for expanding the book's content. Feel free to contact me at:

Dr. Joseph V. Saitta
P.O. Box 5422
Fredericksburg, VA 22403
E-mail: Saitta@aol.com

Acknowledgments

The author would like to acknowledge the assistance of the following people. They all contributed immeasurably to the successful development of this book. Thanks, guys.

John Brown
Ricardo Hernandez Canto
Harold C. Cohen, Ph.D., EMT-P
Joseph M. Dempsey
Jacques Emeriault
John G. Gilliland
David Graham
Dave Grissom, Sr.
Arthur F. Hatch
Dennis Hunter
Kenneth P. Knorr
Steven Kuhr
Ed Lam
Scott Lewis
Kevin Lyles
Sherman Markham
Philip H. McArdle
Jack McCartt
Charlie Miller
George Omohundro
Craig Palmer
Jeff Paullus
Wayne Powell
Dennis Roeding, MAJ, USA (Ret)
Bob See
R. Dale Stanfield
Tommy Terry
David L. Tyler
Michael A. Watson
Kris K. Weiland
Steve White
Gary Williams

Introduction

Overview

This book is divided into three major sections: the Introduction (this chapter), the photographs of the buckles (accompanied by explanatory text in the following chapters), and the final Resources chapter. This introductory chapter contains a definition of terms and many collecting tips. Within the photographic section each chapter is devoted to a single category of belt buckle. For example, the first chapter is on public safety buckles from the world's law enforcement and fire service agencies. The second chapter describes armed forces buckles from around the world. In each of these chapters, the U.S. buckles are presented first within each section, followed by those from the rest of the world. Finally, in the Resources chapter, books and Internet sites are reviewed.

This book provides a comprehensive look at the entire field of men's belt buckle collecting with **one exception**: military buckles that have already been extensively researched. There is no need to duplicate what has already been done (and done quite well) by others. Thus, German Third Reich buckles and those from the American Civil War are generally excluded. However, in the Resources chapter I have included annotated reviews of the "classics" in both of these fields. Further, I have included contact information on some of the many reputable reproduction buckle sellers for those involved in the rapidly growing military reenactment field.

Definitions

A belt buckle is simply a device that has been specially designed to serve as the clasp of a belt. The primary purpose of a belt, of course, is to hold up one's pants. The secondary purpose of a belt and buckle is to provide an opportunity to personalize clothing. So, we have thousands of buckle variations and hundreds of belt variations to choose from. Surprisingly, in countries other than the United States, the buckle of choice for men to wear with casual clothing is the simple frame buckle. Generally, it is devoid of any design. Conversely, in the United States, the buckle of choice for casual wear will most often have a design.

Types of Buckles

Here are definitions of some of the many types of buckles available:

Action: buckles with two or more moving parts. For example, a buckle that depicts the head of a knight wearing a helmet would be considered an action buckle if the helmet visor lifts up.
Badge: buckles with the predominant central design being an agency's badge.

Blanks: buckles with no design or graphic, usually square or rectangular in shape. Also known as "frame" buckles. Except for blanks of some antiquity, there is virtually no collector interest in this buckle type.

Frame Buckles, also known as **blanks**, all modern. No collector interest in these! **Price each:** $5 or less.

Box: buckles, most often manufactured for the German military, that have a box-like appearance. Generally, these are similar in size and shape to a cigarette package. According to Thomas Reid, in his definitive *German Belt Buckles* book (see the Resources chapter for more information), these buckles, also known as "kastenschloesser" (literally "box buckle" in German), have been used by Prussia and Germany since the mid-1800s.

Two Box Buckles.
Top: A common **W.W.I Prussian Army**, enlisted man's brass box buckle, c. 1914, which has been re-painted. Designed for uniform wear. Size 2.5" x 1.75". **Price:** $21 to $40.
Bottom: A **miniature buckle** made to represent a W.W.I Prussian enlisted man's box buckle for use with a child's action figure, such as G.I. Joe®. Currently made in plastic with a white leather belt. Size .75" x .5". **Price:** $5.

Frame: Another name for a "blank" buckle. See "blank" definition above.

Friction: buckles, most often manufactured for the American military, that use a small, internal friction bar (or "roller") to adjust and hold the belt. The common U.S. Army and U.S. Air Force examples have no design and, thus, are not collected. The military services of other countries (usually close allies of America) that use friction buckles generally do add some design to them and these are eagerly collected.

Top: Standard U.S. Army **friction buckle**, brass, c. 1980, designed for uniform wear. Size: 2" x 1.5". **Price:** $5 or less.

Bottom: a U.S. Army friction buckle, brass, c. 1968, uniform wear. The buckle has been modified to be a **short-timer's buckle**: it has not been polished and a large X has been made across the face of the buckle. Size 2" x 1.5". **Price:** $10 or less.

Initial: buckles with no design or minimal design that include an alphabetical letter or letters (usually a maximum of three letters).

Miniature: buckles of extremely small size. These are most often sold for use with children's action figures, such as G.I. Joe®. The level of detail on many of these buckles is quite amazing.

Multi-function: buckles that serve more than the primary function as a belt clasp. For example, a buckle that also holds a gun or a knife is a multi-function buckle.

Multi-function Buckle, wood and fiberglass Touche® Knife, c. 1986, casual wear, made by Gerber Legendary Blades. The knife is held onto the front of the buckle with a stud. Blade size 2", buckle size 2.75" x 1.75". **Price:** $41 to $60.

Short-timer: buckles of the common U.S. Army friction type that were worn with the fatigue uniform by soldiers whose enlistments were almost over. Traditionally, these buckles were not polished and often had the addition of hand-crafted designs or sayings. It is doubtful that the tradition continues since the fatigue uniform has been replaced by the battle dress utility uniform which is often worn with a large frame buckle and a nylon belt.

Two-piece: buckles composed of two interlocking parts. Also known as "spoon" buckles due to the shape of one of the pieces. In England, when these are used with military uniforms, they are also referred to as "waist belt clasps."

British South Wales Borderers (Other Ranks) **two-piece** buckle (or waist belt clasp), chrome, age unknown, uniform wear. Size 3" x 2.5". **Price:** $20 or less.

Western: buckles that are usually in an oval shape with a rope-edged border and some type of western-related center design.

Western-style buckle of pewter with enamel, c. 1998, casual wear. Size 3.5" x 2.5". **Price:** $20 or less.

In addition to the types of buckles, it is also helpful to know when buckles are worn. I have tried to categorize the buckles in this book into one of three classifications:

Casual: buckles meant for wear with non-uniform clothing. These are the opposite of uniform buckles.

Uniform: buckles authorized for wear with an official uniform. These can be agency-provided or privately purchased. These are the opposite of casual buckles.

Unknown: buckles that could not be determined as definitely meant for either casual wear or for uniform wear. If you can clear up these "mysteries," please contact me.

Generally, photo captions throughout the book will include notations that indicate whether the buckles are for casual, uniform, or unknown wear.

Collecting Tips

Finding Buckles

If you're like most belt buckle collectors, you're probably always on the lookout for more of them. Commercial sources are, of course, a good starting point. Several of the better-known companies are listed in the Resources chapter. However, other reasonably priced sources exist as well.

For example, some of my most consistently productive sources for buckles are garage sales, flea markets, and gun shows. I don't believe that I've ever gone to one of these without returning with at least one or two "prizes." Usually, buckles at these sources will also be **extremely** low priced, with $3 to $8 being the average price range for a single buckle.

A group of buckles purchased at a 1999 gun show: one in pewter, the rest in brass. **Average price:** $5.

Want free buckles? Well, they're out there…for the asking. Yep, your relatives and friends have accumulated many buckles over their lifetimes and would be more than happy to give them to you. I'll even admit to asking my own sons to "loan" me buckles for use in this book. As I started to write this book, I needed to "flesh out" several chapters. Overall, I was approximately 100 buckles shy of the total needed. Over half of those 100 buckles were provided by family and friends. The lesson: let people know that you're interested in collecting belt buckles.

The Internet is also a productive source for buckles. I've purchased several buckles this way. The range of prices is from a low of $5 per buckle to a high of $20 per buckle, excluding postage. Multiple buckle "deals" are often extremely reasonable. I recall a recent eBay® auction for 37 The Buckle Works (TBW) law enforcement buckles that were sold to the high bidder for $68, plus postage. Individually, these high-quality buckles would retail for at least $15 each.

At this stage in this budding hobby there is no national association of belt buckle collectors. Nor is there a single newsletter or magazine that exclusively addresses how to locate buckles or identify them. Instead you will find that acquiring information about buckles and how to obtain them requires some detective work from a variety of sources. In the Resources chapter I've included brief reviews of some of the limited numbers of books, Internet sites, and other leads on buckles.

Prices

Collecting belt buckles is not usually about making investment decisions. Rather, it is about having fun, so collect what you like. Fortunately, collecting buckles also normally won't bust your budget. For example, about 75% of the buckles in this book originally cost less than $20, with many costing less than $10. At the other end of the spectrum, there are a handful of buckles in this book that originally cost between $75 and $100. They were obtained directly from commercial sources. Again, these represent an exception, and the "high end" of my collection.

Naturally, there are also exceptions to the low-priced buckles that comprise the bulk of most people's collections. If you decide that you want to collect a few World War II German buckles from elite units, prices will shift to the hundreds, or even thousands, of dollars. Or, perhaps, you decide to put together a collection composed solely of buckles made from solid gold or sterling silver. Then you will be spending some serious dollars. But, there are many high quality **and** low-priced buckles "out there" just waiting for you to give them a home.

Of course, a buckle is only worth what you are willing to pay for it. But, here are a few pointers on the types of buckles that are usually expensive:

1. Those made from precious metals and/or embedded with gemstones
2. Buckles with a historic, documented connection to a famous person
3. Uniform buckles from WWII German military organizations
4. Uniform buckles from the American Civil War, especially from the Confederate forces
5. Ones from countries that no longer exist as political entities (for example, a South Vietnamese Military Academy buckle)
6. Strictly-controlled buckles from small, elite military or police organizations (for example, a Republic of South Africa 32nd Battalion's Unit buckle)

7. Combinations of the above (a Rhodesian Special Air Service buckle – which is an example of numbers 5 and 6).

Unfortunately, another factor that complicates the purchase of some of the above buckles is that they have been reproduced. This is especially true of numbers 2, 3, and 4 above. There's a saying in the police badge collecting field that's appropriate to buckle collecting: "First, you buy the book, then you buy the badge." Just insert the word "buckle" for "badge" and you've got the idea. Before purchasing expensive buckles, take the time to research them. Again, the Resources chapter of this book contains reviews of some of the most helpful books that deal with "high end" buckles.

As for the prices in this book, they are the actual original purchase prices of the buckles, adjusted to current replacement dollars, as necessary. By "replacement dollars" I mean what the buckle would cost if purchased today. The adjustments were based on recent actual auction and sales prices, and/or suggested retail prices. If a buckle was a "freebie" (a gift from a relative or friend), I have listed an approximation of the actual purchase price, also adjusted to current replacement dollars. Since the price of a buckle depends, to some extent, on condition, I have provided a range of prices for each buckle (for example, $21-$40). The low dollar figure represents a buckle in average condition (it has been used, but there are no large scratches that detract from the appearance of the buckle, and the plating is not worn through) while the high dollar figure represents a buckle in mint, unworn condition.

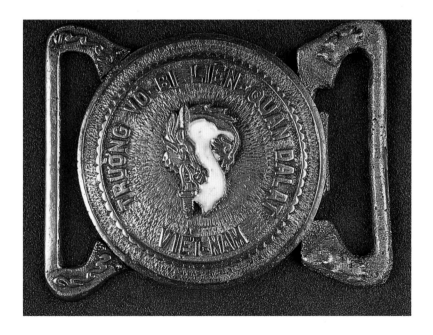

Public Safety Buckles

Overview

Collecting public safety items is a long established hobby. However, public safety buckles have not yet received the collecting attention given to cloth patches, metal badges, pins, hats, and other such things. By "public safety" I mean those agencies, worldwide, that provide law enforcement, fire protection, and pre-hospital emergency medical services (EMS). In the United States, these include police and sheriff's departments, military police agencies, fire departments, and EMS agencies, both paid and volunteer.

Law Enforcement

Federal agencies with police or intelligence functions, state police and highway patrol organizations, local municipal police or sheriff's departments, law enforcement associations, and private security or training companies—they're all part of law enforcement. Municipal police departments in America are estimated to number about 18,000 agencies, most quite small (50 members or less).

In this section American law enforcement agencies' buckles are presented first, sub-divided into the buckles of federal agencies, state police and highway patrol organizations, local police and sheriff's departments, law enforcement associations, and private security or training companies. Foreign law enforcement agencies' buckles are then presented.

Federal Agencies

National Reconnaissance Office, United States of America, chrome with enamel, c. 1997, casual wear. Size 2.5" x 1.5". This rather ordinary looking friction buckle is actually for an organizational division of the Central Intelligence Agency. **Price:** $41 to $60.

Three excellent federal buckles.
Top: U.S. Marine Corps Military Police
Bottom left: U.S. Department of Agriculture
Bottom right: U.S. Department of State
All three are in brass, and 3.5" x 2.5" in size. **Price range:** $21 to $60.

Central Intelligence Agency, brass, c. 1999, casual wear. Size 3.5" x 2.5". **Price:** $41 to $60.

United States Secret Service, brass, c. 1988, casual wear. Size 3" x 2". The back of the buckle includes an inscription that manufacture was "Authorized by the Uniform Division, U.S. Secret Service." Note that the correct name of the organization is the Uniform**ed** Division. The Secret Service was formed in 1922. The Uniformed Division was originally known as the White House Police. **Price:** $41 to $60.

United States Secret Service, brass, c. 1988, casual wear. Size 2.75" in diameter. The back of this buckle also includes an inscription that manufacture was "Authorized by the Uniform Division, U.S. Secret Service." See note in previous photo's caption about the correct name of the organization. **Price:** $41 to $60.

U.S. Army Military Police, brass, c. 1990, casual wear. Size 3.5" x 2.5". The crossed pistols in the center design are, in fact, the U. S. Army Military Police's branch of service insignia. However, the skull with helmet, and the motto ("Kick Ass & Take Names") are *very* unofficial. **Price:** $21 to $40.

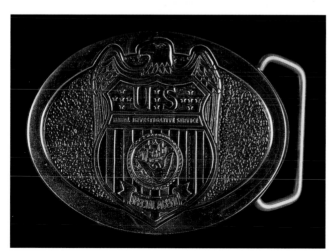

U.S. Naval Investigative Service, brass, c. 1988, casual wear. Size 3.5" x 2.5". Originally this service was known as the Office of Naval Intelligence and formed in 1916. **Price:** $20 or less.

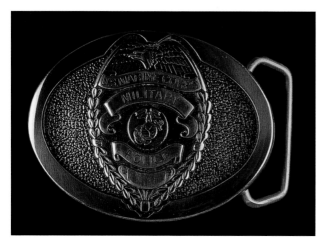

U. S. Marine Corps Military Police, brass, c. 1992, casual wear. Size 3.5" x 2.5". This finely crafted buckle, like many others in this chapter, features the organization's badge as its central design. **Price:** $21 to $40.

U.S. Air Force, Security Police, brass, c. 1994, casual wear. Size 3.5" x 2.5". With the separation of the Army Air Corps from the U.S. Army in 1947, the Security Police (then known as "Air Police") were formed as a component of the new U.S. Air Force. **Price:** $20 or less.

Drug Enforcement Administration, brass, c. 1986, casual wear. Size 3.5" x 2.5". Tracing its evolution back to 1914, when it was part of the Bureau of the Revenue, the Drug Enforcement Administration has gone through several organizational and name changes. In 1968, it was transferred from the Treasury Department into the Justice Department. **Price:** $21 to $40.

Department of State, Office of Security, brass, c. 1984, casual wear. Size 3.5" x 2.5". Special Agents of this agency perform a variety of functions including protecting the Secretary of State. **Price:** $21 to $40.

Internal Revenue Service, Criminal Investigation Division, brass, c. 1982, casual wear. Size 3.5" x 2.5". These agents conduct criminal investigations involving tax fraud and evasion. Al Capone was one of their early successful prosecutions **Price:** $21 to $40.

Revenue Cutter Service, brass, a reproduction of a buckle worn c. 1900, unknown current wear, but originally worn with the uniform. Size 2.75" x 2". This is a well-crafted reproduction by Hanover Brass Foundry, Mechanicsville, Virginia. The Revenue Cutter Service was the forerunner of the Internal Revenue Service. **Price:** $20 or less.

United States Border Patrol, brass, c. 1992, casual wear. Size 3.5" x 2.5". The Border Patrol is the uniformed enforcement arm of the Immigration and Naturalization Service. **Price:** $20 or less.

United States Border Patrol, brass, c. 1994, casual wear. Size 3.5" x 2.5". This buckle illustrates an earlier Border Patrol badge. **Price:** $20 or less.

United States Border Patrol, brass, c. 1994, casual wear. Size 3.5" x 2.5". This buckle celebrates the founding of the Border Patrol in 1924. **Price:** $20 or less.

Immigration and Naturalization Service, brass, c. 1992, casual wear. Size 3.5" x 1.75". The Service was established in 1864 as part of the Department of State. **Price:** $21 to $40.

FBI National Academy, pewter, c. 1986, casual wear. Size 3" x 2.25". The FBI National Academy trains state and local law enforcement personnel. **Price:** $20 or less.

National Park Service, brass, c. 1981, casual wear. Size 2.5" x 1.75". The back of this buckle includes a statement that it was produced for the Ranger Association of the Yosemite (California) National Park. **Price:** $20 or less.

Department of Agriculture, Veterinary Medical Service, Meat and Poultry Inspector, brass, c. 1994, casual wear. Size 3.5" x 2.5". This is a fairly rare buckle. **Price:** $41 to $60.

State Police and Highway Patrol Agencies

These buckles represent many fine **State Police and Highway Patrol** departments. All are of brass, c. 1985 to 1999. **Prices** for each range from a low of $20 to a high of $40.

Alaska State Trooper, brass, c. 1996, casual wear. Size 3.5" x 2.5". The bear's head topped badge is unique to Alaska. **Price:** $41 to $60.

Arkansas State Police, pewter, c. 1994, casual wear. Size 3" x 2". **Price:** $20 or less.

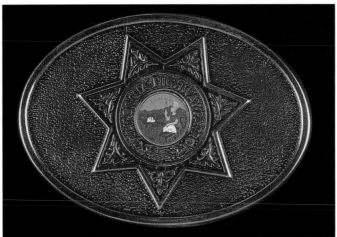

California Highway Patrol, brass with enamel center, c. 1997, casual wear. Size 3.5" x 2.5". **Price:** $21 to $40.

Georgia State Patrol, brass, c. 1992, casual wear. Size 3.5" x 2.5". **Price:** $21 to $40.

Maine State Police, brass, c. 1994, casual wear. Size 2.75" x 2". **Price:** $20 or less.

Maryland State Police, brass with enamel center, c. 1998, uniform wear. Size 2.75" x 1.75". **Price:** $41 to $60.

Maryland State Police, 50th Anniversary, brass, c. 1985, casual wear. Size 3.5" x 2.5". **Price:** $21 to $40.

Michigan State Police, brass with enamel center, c. 1988, casual wear. Size 3.5" x 2.5". **Price:** $20 or less.

Montana Highway Patrol, brass, c. 1999, casual wear. Size 3.5" x 2.5". In days gone by, the numbers at the bottom of the buckle, 3-7-77, had some secret meaning. Unfortunately, no one seems to now know exactly what the meaning was. **Price:** $21 to $40.

Two outstanding buckles produced by the Montana Silversmiths Company of Columbus, Montana. **Top:** Montana Highway Patrol Association **Bottom:** Montana Highway Patrol Both are chrome with brass, c. 1999, casual wear. Size of each is 4"x 3". **Price each:** $61 to $80.

Oregon State Police, brass, c. 1995, casual wear. Size 3.5" x 2.25". **Price:** $21 to $40.

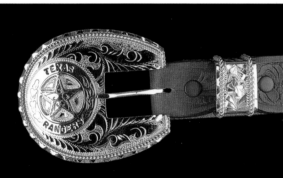

Texas Rangers, chrome with brass detail, c. 1999, uniform wear. Size 3" x 2.25". This buckle comes as a four piece set with a buckle, belt tip, and two loops (one of which is shown in the photo). The set is made by Mark Smith, a prisoner in the Texas state prison system. Chuck Norris wears one of these buckles in the television show *Walker: Texas Ranger*. **Price:** $121 to $140.

Utah Highway Patrol, brass, c. 1992, casual wear. Size 3.5" x 2.25". **Price:** $21 to $40.

Wyoming Highway Patrol, bonded marble, c. 1998, casual wear. Size 3.5" x 2.25". Celebrating the Patrol's 25th anniversary. **Price:** $20 or less.

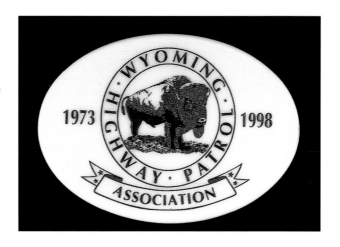

Police and Sheriff's Departments

COBRA Team, pewter, c. 1985, casual wear. Size 3.25" x 2.25". "COBRA" is an acronym for "Combined Outlaw Biker Research and Attack." Unknown jurisdiction. **Price:** $41 to $60.

Metropolitan Police, Washington, D.C., brass, c. 1982, casual wear. Size 2" x 2". This buckle is an excellent depiction of this department's badge, although it is somewhat smaller in size. **Price:** $21 to $40.

Metropolitan Police, Washington, D.C., 125th Anniversary, brass, c. 1986, casual wear. Size 3" x 2". The Metropolitan Police Department was organized in 1861. **Price:** $21 to $40.

Metropolitan Police, Washington, D.C., brass, c. 1976, casual wear. Size 3.25" x 2.5". Since this buckle is much older than the others made for this department, the quality is, unfortunately, not as high. **Price:** $20 or less.

Bibb County, Georgia, Sheriff's Department, brass, c. 1988, casual wear. Size 3.5" x 2.5". Notice the many small bubbles on the surface of this buckle. These are indicators of an improper casting process. **Price:** $10 or less.

Training Academy, Marion County, Indiana, brass, age unknown, casual wear. Size 3" x 2". Produced for the Marion County Sheriff's Department's Training Academy. **Price:** $20 or less.

Prince George's County, Maryland, Sheriff's Office, 300th Anniversary, brass, c. 1996, casual wear. Size 3.5" x 2.5". Now, this *exceptionally* high quality buckle is from a *really* old department, by American standards! **Price:** $41 to $60.

26

Deputy Sheriff, Saginaw County, Michigan, brass and chrome, c. 1987, casual wear. Size 3.5" x 2.5". Definitely different: a western-type buckle from Michigan. **Price:** $21 to $40.

Ballwin Police Department, Missouri, brass, c. 1998, casual wear. Size 3.5" x 2.5". **Price:** $20 or less.

New York Police Department, New York, brass, c. 1986, casual wear. Size 3.5" x 2.5". Some of New York City's well-known features are included on this buckle, including the Statue of Liberty and the twin towers of the World Trade Center. **Price:** $21 to $40.

Richland, Washington, Police Department, brass, age unknown, casual wear. Size 3" x 2". **Price:** $20 or less.

Milwaukee, Wisconsin, Police Department, pewter, c. 1992, casual wear. Size 2" in diameter. **Price:** $20 or less.

Buckle Up Award, Mesquite, Arizona, Police Department, brass with enamel center, c. 1994, casual wear. Size 3" x 2". Police in this jurisdiction would stop motorists who were wearing their seat belts and give them these buckles as an award. Great idea! **Price:** $20 or less.

Miscellaneous U.S. Law Enforcement

International Association of Bomb Technicians and Investigators, copper over base metal, age unknown, casual wear. Size 3.5" x 2.5". **Price:** $21 to $40.

Member, Society of Explosives Engineers, brass, age unknown, casual wear. Size 2.5" in diameter. **Price:** $20 or less.

City of New York Police Benevolent Association, pewter with enamel center, c. 1997, casual wear. Size 3" x 2.5". **Price:** $20 or less.

Police Benevolent Association, location unknown, brass, age unknown, casual wear. Size 3" x 2". **Price:** $21 to $40.

Blue Knights, Law Enforcement Motorcycle Club, Inc., France 1, location unknown, pewter, c. 1993, casual wear. Size 3.5" x 2.5". **Price:** $21 to $40.

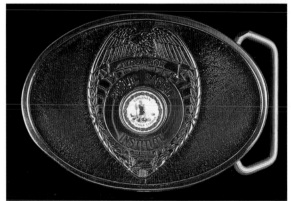

Director, Public Safety Institute, Sterling, Virginia, brass with enamel Virginia state seal, c. 1982, casual wear. Size 3.5" x 2.5". **Price:** $20 or less.

Pinkerton Special Service, location unknown, chrome with enamel, age unknown, uniform wear. Size 2.75" x 1.75". **Price:** $20 or less.

Police, generic, chrome, a one piece reproduction of a two piece buckle made in the late 1800s, originally for uniform wear. Size 3" x 2". **Price:** $21 to $40.

American Lawman, generic, pewter, c. 1986, casual wear. Size 3.5" x 2.5". **Price:** $20 or less.

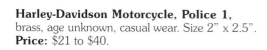

Harley-Davidson Motorcycle, Police 1, brass, age unknown, casual wear. Size 2" x 2.5". **Price:** $21 to $40.

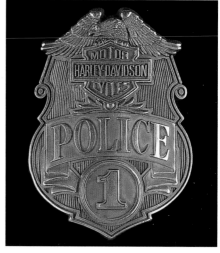

Police, America's Finest, generic, pewter with enamel, c. 1988, casual wear. Size 3.25" x 2.25". **Price:** $20 or less.

Patience, Integrity, Guts, PIG, brass, c. 1975, casual wear. Size 3.25" x 2.5". The 1960s hippie term for police, pig, has been converted by cops into a working creed: patience, integrity, guts. **Price:** $21 to $40.

Florida Police, generic, brass, c. 1994, casual wear. Size 3.5" x 2.75". **Price:** $20 or less.

Foreign Law Enforcement

Gendarmerie Imperiale, Surete Publique (France), brass, from the French Imperial era, uniform wear. This double die piece is of extremely high quality. Size 3.75" x 3". **Price:** $121 to $140.

Garde Republicaine (France), brass, age unknown, uniform wear. Size 2.5" x 2.75". The Garde performs special assignments in Paris, such as VIP protection. The City of Paris seal is the center design. **Price:** $41 to $60.

Gendarmerie Ordre Public (France), brass, age unknown, uniform wear. Size 2.75" x 2.75". **Price:** $41 to $60.

French Police, chrome with portion of the white plastic belt attached, c. 1990, uniform wear. Size 2" x 2". **Price:** $20 or less.

German Police, Enlisted, aluminum, World War II era, uniform wear. Size 2.5" x 1.75". The motto "Gott mit uns" translates as "God is with us." **Price:** $101 to $120.

Saxony Police, Germany, steel, age unknown, uniform wear. Size 2.5" x 2". **Price:** $41 to $60.

Gendarmerie, Vaud (Switzerland), brass, c. 1971, uniform wear. Size 3" x 1.75". **Price:** $21 to $40.

Netherlands Police, chrome with enamel, current, uniform wear. The blue nylon belt is attached. Size 3" x 2". **Price:** $21 to $40.

Canadian Provost Corps,
brass, c. 1976, uniform wear.
Size 3.5" x 2.75". **Price:** $21 to
$40.

**Royal Canadian Mounted
Police (Canada),** brass friction
style with enamel, c. 1997,
unknown wear. Size 2.75" x 1.5".
Price: $21 to $40.

**Royal Canadian Mounted
Police (Canada),** brass with
enamel, c. 1999, casual wear.
Size 3" x 2.5". **Price:** $21 to
$40.

**Royal Canadian Mounted
Police (Canada),** pewter, c. 1996,
casual wear. Size 3" x 2". **Price:**
$20 or less.

**Police Montreal
(Canada),** brass, c.
1988, uniform wear.
Size 4" x 2.75".
Price: $21 to $40.

**Ontario Provincial Police
(Canada),** brass, c. 1997, unknown
wear. Size 2.25" x 1.75". **Price:** $20
or less.

**Ministry of the
Interior Police
(USSR),** brass, c.
1985, uniform wear.
Size 3" x 2". **Price:**
$41 to $60.

Ministry of the Interior Police (State of Russia), brass, c. 2000, uniform wear. Size 2.75" x 2". The center seal is the Imperial era double-headed eagle, which is used by the current government. **Price:** $41 to $60.

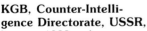

Traffic Police/ Inspectors (GAI of the USSR) **Top left:** Actual badge used by GAI, base metal with enamel, c. 1985, uniform wear. Size 2.75" x 4". **Price:** $41 to $60.

Bottom right: Buckle made in the U.S. replicating the GAI badge, brass and enamel, c. 1999, casual wear. The quality of the buckle is *better* than the badge. Size 2.25" x 3.25". **Price:** $21 to $40.

KGB, Counter-Intelligence Directorate, USSR, brass, c. 1988, unknown wear. Size 3" x 2". A mystery: if this buckle was for uniform wear it must have been just before the fall of the Soviet Union. As for casual wear, why would anyone wear the buckle of the dreaded "Organs of State?" Yet, minute scratches on both the front and back of the buckle indicate that it has been worn. **Price:** $61 to $80.

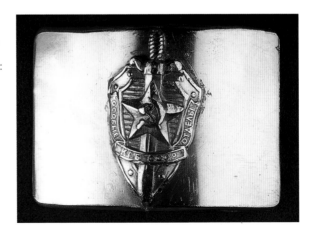

British South Africa Police, brass two-piece buckle, c. 1979, uniform wear. Size 3.5" x 2.25". **Price:** $41 to $60.

Two British South Africa Police buckles, brass two-piece, c. 1970s, uniform wear. Notice the subtle differences in size and detail. **Price each:** $41 to $60.

British South Africa Police, chrome two-piece buckle, age unknown, uniform wear. Size 3.5" x 2.25". Compared to the previous BSAP buckles, this has a different center seal and "British South Africa Police" in both English and Afrikaans. **Price:** $41 to $60.

Three African Police buckles, all are chrome two-piece, c. 1980s, uniform wear. The buckle on the right is missing the center section (or "spoon"). Locating a replacement would be very difficult. **Price** of buckle on the right: $10 or less. **Price** of other two buckles: $41 to $60.

Zambia Police (Africa), chrome two-piece, c. 1986, uniform wear. Size 4" x 2.25". **Price:** $41 to $60.

Administration Police (Kenya, Africa), chrome two-piece, c. 1989, uniform wear. Size 4" x 2.25". **Price:** $41 to $60.

Yugoslavia Military Police, chrome with brass and enamel, c. 1981, uniform wear. Size 2.75" x 2.5". **Price:** $21 to $40.

39

Norway Police, brass two-piece, c. 1992, uniform wear. Size 3.5" x 1.75". **Price:** $21 to $40.

Macedonia Military Police, chrome, c. 1997, uniform wear. Size 2" x 2". **Price:** $21 to $40.

El Salvador National Police, brass, c. 1993, uniform wear. Size 2.75" x 2". **Price:** $21 to $40.

Victoria Police (Australia), chrome with enamel, c. 1998, uniform wear. Size 2.5" x 2". **Price:** $20 or less.

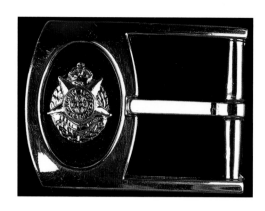

Tasmania Police (Australia), brass with enamel, c. 1996, uniform wear. Size 2.5" x 2". **Price:** $20 or less.

Queensland Police (Australia), chrome with enamel, c. 2000, uniform wear. Size 2.5" x 2". **Price:** $20 or less.

New Zealand Police, chrome with enamel, c. 1998, uniform wear. Size 2.5" x 2". **Price:** $20 or less.

Justice Police (Republic of Vietnam), chrome two-piece, c. 1968, uniform wear. Size 3.5" x 2.75". The motto, "Cong Minh Liem Chinh," at the bottom of the buckle translates as "Justice and Honor." **Price:** $101 to $120.

Saigon Police (Republic of Vietnam), chrome with leather belt attached, c. 1968, unknown wear. Size 2" x 1.25". **Price:** $61 to $80.

Gong An (People's Republic of China Police), chrome friction buckle with brass and enamel, c. 2000, unknown wear. Size 3" x 1.75". **Price:** $21 to $40.

Thailand Police, brass, c. 1988, uniform wear. Size 2" x 1.5". **Price:** $20 or less.

Malaysia Police, chrome, c. 1985, uniform wear. Size 2" x 1.25". **Price:** $20 or less.

Fire Service

The range of services of fire departments has expanded considerably over the last 30 years. Modern departments, around the world, provide fire suppression, prevention, hazardous materials response, public education, specialized rescue (confined space and high angle rescue, for example), arson investigation, emergency medical services (EMS), etc. In the United States there are approximately 34,000 fire departments with about 75% of those being volunteer organizations.

The buckles in this section are shown in the following order: American fire departments and organizations (including associations), and then foreign departments. Red Cross buckles are included in the foreign group since only two, both German, were available. It was also my intention to include buckles of civil defense (or as it is now known, "emergency management") agencies. However, the only one that came to hand was a World War II German Reichsluftschutzbund (National Air Protection Association) buckle in poor condition. Perhaps in a future edition that situation can be rectified.

American Fire Departments

National Fire Academy, wood, c. 1982, casual wear. Size 3.75" x 2.5". Routed into the center of the buckle is the Academy's "Hotfoot" eagle logo. **Price:** $21 to $40

National Fire Academy, Adjunct Faculty, brass, c. 1988, casual wear. Size 3.5" x 2.5". The Adjunct Faculty is the Academy's contract instructor cadre. **Price:** $21 to $40.

National Fire Academy, brass, c. 1982, casual wear. Size 3" x 2.5". **Price:** $21 to $40.

Silent Hero, Firefighter, chrome and brass, c. 1988, casual wear. Size 4" x 3.5". Designed for the Firefighters' Olympics by R. Dale Stanfield, Bullhead City, Arizona. **Price:** $61 to $80.

Grouping of Four Fire Buckles, all are of recent manufacture, casual wear. **Price each:** $21 to $40. **Top left:** Bethesda, Maryland **Top right:** Charlottesville, Virginia **Bottom left:** Flagstaff, Arizona **Bottom right:** St. Louis, Missouri.

Shreveport (Louisiana) Fire Department, 150th Anniversary, brass, c. 1987, casual wear. Size 3.5"x 2.75". **Price:** $21 to $40.

America's Heroes, Boston Fire Department, brass, c. 1985, casual wear. Size 4" x 2.75". **Price:** $21 to $40.

Top left: America's Firefighters, pewter and enamel generic buckle, c. 1983, casual wear. Size 3.5"x 2.25". **Price:** $20 or less.

Top right: Assistant Chief, brass and enamel generic buckle, c. 1977, casual wear. Size 3" x 2". **Price:** $20 or less.

Bottom left: Hazardous Materials Response Teams, 15th Anniversary, June 4-7, 1998, bronze over base metal, c. 1998. Size 3" x 2". **Price:** $21 to $40.

Bottom right: Fire Department, City of New York, The Bravest, base metal with brass and chrome finish, c. 1988, casual wear. Size 4" x 2.75". Buckle's plating is starting to wear off. **Price:** $20 or less.

Mukwonago (Wisconsin), Place of the Bear, pewter, c. 1988, casual wear. Size 3" x 2.75". **Price:** $21 to $40.

North Pole, Alaska, Fire Department, brass and chrome, c. 1998, casual wear. Size 3.5" x 2.5". **Price:** $41 to $60.

**Mountain View (California)
Firefighters Local 1965,**
brass, c. 1986, casual wear.
Size 3" x 2.25". **Price:** $21 to
$40.

Top left: Texas Fire Fighters, Lubbock,
1983, sterling silver, c. 1990, casual
wear. Size 3.75" x 2.75". **Price:** $81 to
$100.
Top right: Grapevine (Texas) Fire
Department, brass, c. 1985, casual wear.
Size 3.75" x 2.5". **Price:** $21 to $40.
Bottom left: Ketchikan (Alaska) Fire
Department, brass, c. 1981, casual wear.
Size 3.5" x 2.5". **Price:** $21 to $40.
Bottom right: South Dakota Fire
Service, brass, c. 1984, casual wear. Size
3.25" x 2.5". Price: $21 to $40.

Three Named Buckles. Some fire departments allow the option of wearing a privately-
purchased buckle with the firefighter's name included as part of the design.
Top left: "George" with Fairfax County, Virginia, seal in upper right corner, brass with
enamel, c. 1980, uniform wear. Size 3" x 1.75". **Price:** $20 or less.
Top right: "Art" with Sunriver, Oregon, logo in upper right corner, chrome with enamel,
c. 1988, uniform wear. Size 2.75" x 1.75". **Price:** $20 or less.
Bottom center: "H. C. Cohen'" with "Balto County (Maryland) F. D.," brass, c. 1997,
uniform wear. Size .2.75" x 1.75" **Price:** $20 or less.

Bottom left: LSU Fireman Training, brushed brass finish, c. 1988, casual wear. Size 2.5" x 2.5". **Price:** $20 or less.

Top right: Certified Smoke Diver, State Fire Academy, Mississippi, pewter, c. 1998, casual wear. This Academy's Smoke Diver course is particularly demanding. Size 2.5" x 2.5". **Price:** $20 or less.

Left: Maugansville Goodwill Volunteer Fire Company (Maryland), brass and enamel, c. 1996, casual wear. Size 3.25" x 2.5". **Price:** $20 or less.

Right: Gloucester County (New Jersey) Fire Training Graduate, brass with enamel, c. 1985, casual wear. Size 2.5" in diameter. **Price:** $20 or less.

Virginia Society of Fire Service Instructors, brass, c. 1993, casual wear. Size 3.5" x 2.25". **Price:** $20 or less.

Top: Los Angeles City Fire Department, brass, c. 1985, casual wear. Size 3.75" x 3". **Price:** $21 to $40. **Bottom:** LAFD, chrome, c. 1987, privately-purchased, but used for uniform wear. Size 1.5" x 2". **Price:** $20 or less.

Two well-designed buckles for the Renton, Washington, Firefighters Local.
Left: chrome, c. 1998, casual wear. Size 3"x 2.25". **Price:** $21 to $40.
Right: brass, c. 1989, casual wear. Size 3.25" x 2.25". **Price:** $21 to $40.

Two Florida Fire Service buckles.
Top: Tampa Fire Department, 1895-1995, brass, c. 1995, casual wear. Size 3.25"x 2.25". **Price:** $21 to $40.
Right: Boca Raton Firefighters (Local) 1560, brass with enamel, c. 1990, casual wear. Size 2.75" x 2". **Price:** $21 to $40.

Emergency Medical Services (EMS).
Top left: Colorado Paramedic, pewter, c. 1987, casual wear. Size 3"x 2.5".
Price: $20 or less.
Top right: EMT (Emergency Medical Technician), brass, c. 1977, casual wear. Size 3.25" x 2.25". **Price:** $21 to $40.
Bottom left: Emergency Medical Service, A System to Save a Life, brass with enamel, c. 1982, casual wear. Size 3.5" x 2.75". **Price:** $20 or less.
Bottom right: Paramedic, pewter, c. 1986, casual wear. Size 2.75"x 2". **Price:** $20 or less.

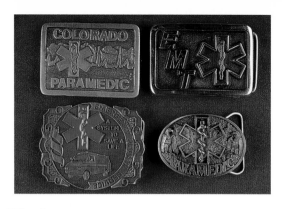

Two more EMS buckles.
Left: brass over base metal, c. 1978, casual wear. The buckle uses the "Star of Life" design. Size 2.75" in diameter. **Price:** $20 or less
Right: brass over base metal, c. 1972, casual wear. Size 2.5" in diameter. This buckle uses the U.S. Army's Medical Corps symbol, the caduceus, as its design. **Price:** $21 to $40.

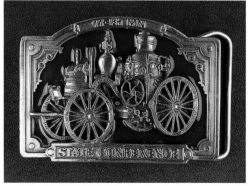

International Association of Firefighters, brass with enamel, c. 1987, casual wear. Size 3" x 2". **Price:** $20 or less.

113th MN State Conference, pewter with enamel, c. 1985, casual wear. Size 3" x 2.25". **Price:** $21 to $40.

This Bud's® For You, The American Firefighter, pewter with enamel, c. 1987, casual wear. Part of a series of tribute buckles by Anheuser-Busch, Inc. Size 3" x 2.5". **Price:** $21 to $40.

Fire Engineering (Magazine), Since 1877, brass, c. 1997, casual wear. Size 3" x 2". **Price:** $20 or less.

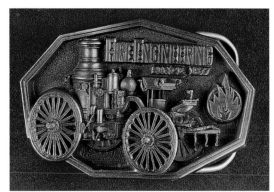

Two generic buckles.
Left: I'm Proud to be an American Fire Fighter, pewter, c. 1986, casual wear. Size 3" x 2". **Price:** $20 or less.
Right: Search and Rescue, pewter, c. 1997, casual wear. Size 3.25" x 2.25". **Price:** $20 or less.

An Open Cab Fire Truck, pewter, c. 1981, casual wear. Size 4.25" x 2". **Price:** $20 or less.

Foreign Fire Departments

Czech Republic Fireman, chrome two piece dress buckle, c. 1997, uniform wear. Size 3.5" x 1.75". **Price:** $41 to $60.

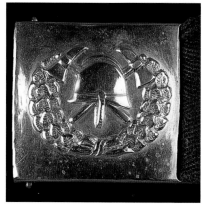

Czech Republic Fireman, chrome friction buckle for wear with work uniform, c. 1993, Size 1.75" x 1.5". **Price:** $20 or less.

Two French fire buckles, brass on the left, chrome on the right, c. 1995, uniform wear. "Sapeurs Pompiers" translates as "Fireman." Size 2.5" x 2.5". **Price each:** $21 to $40.

Army Fire Service (England), chrome two piece with attached belt, current era (Queen Elizabeth II), uniform wear. Size 3.5" x 3". **Price:** $41 to $60.

British Fireman, generic, chrome, c. 1998, casual wear. Size 3.25" x 2.5". This is a rare one since, generally, casual wear buckles are an American phenomena. **Price:** $21 to $40.

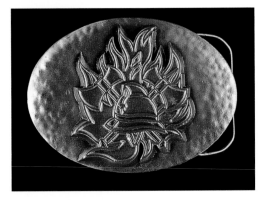

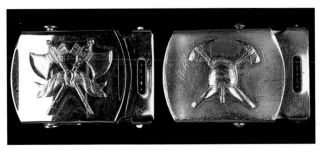

Republic of South Africa Fire Service, two friction buckles, uniform wear. Size 2.25" x 1.5". The buckle on the left is in current use, while the one on the right is of older vintage. **Price each:** $20 or less.

Republic of South Africa (RSA) Fire Service, chrome stable belt buckle, c. 1990, uniform wear. This appears to be a two piece buckle, but is actually constructed as a solid unit. Size 5" x 2.75". **Price:** $21 to $40.

Pretoria Fire Service (RSA), brass, c. 1995, unknown wear. The center design is of a Hurst® extrication tool. Size 3.75" x 2.75". **Price:** $21 to $40.

Republic of South Africa (RSA), chrome stable belt buckle, c. 1990, uniform wear. This may be a fire service buckle or for a separate ambulance service. RSA is unique in using a red "Star of Life," which is usually blue. Size 4" x 2.75". **Price:** $21 to $40.

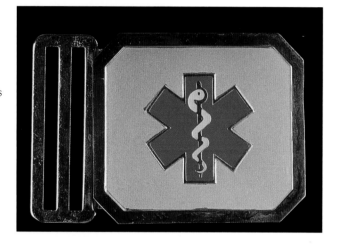

Japanese Fire Service, brass two piece buckle, c. 1980, uniform wear. Size 2.75" x 1.75". **Price:** $41 to $60.

Malaysia Fire Service, chrome with enamel friction buckle, c. 1988, uniform wear. Size 2.25" x 1.5". **Price:** $20 or less.

Fire Services, Hong Kong, brass, c. 1996, casual wear. Size 3.5" x 2.5". Since Hong Kong is now part of the People's Republic of China, the central design has changed. It now has replaced the crown. **Price:** $61 to $80.

New Zealand Fire Service, brass with enamel and pewter, c. 1994, unknown wear. Size 3.5" x 2.5". **Price:** $20 or less.

East German (DDR) Fire Service, chrome box buckle, c. 1988, uniform wear. Size 2.5" x 1.75". **Price:** $21 to $40.

Two German Fire Service buckles. Both are of the box buckle style and for uniform wear. Both are 2.5" x 2". The motto on both, "Gott Zur Ehr Dem Nachsten zur Wehr," translates as "God protect the next ones called to duty."
Left: Current model, but the design dates back to at least W.W.II. Chromed steel with a silver-colored center seal. **Price:** $21 to $40.
Right: World War II era buckle, chromed steel with a brass center seal. **Price:** $41 to $60.

German Red Cross.
Top left: World War II enlisted. Note the swastika in the center of the eagle's chest. Aluminum box buckle, uniform wear. Size 2.5" x 1.75". **Price:** $101 to $120
Bottom right: Current model, brass with enamel center, uniform wear. Size: 3.5" x 2". **Price:** $21 to $40.

Military Buckles

Overview

Historically, the military forces have split their working lives into two very different worlds. The first is all spit and polish, with parades on beautiful spring days, that showcase marching troops in immaculate uniforms with medals gleaming, as bands play martial airs. The second is blood and mud, the sound of explosions, dead buddies, and fear. Each world is historically important, and you'll find buckles from both worlds presented here.

The organization of buckles in this chapter is by types of military organization. U.S. Army buckles (issue and otherwise) are shown, followed by those of foreign armies. In some cases I could not determine if the buckle was from a country that had consolidated the armed forces or a nation that maintained separate branches for the Army, Navy, etc. In those cases, such buckles were included with the foreign **armies** buckles. Next in line are those buckles of the U.S. Navy and of foreign navies. The few U.S. Air Force and foreign air forces buckles available are presented as one section. These are followed by the U.S. Marine Corps and foreign Marine Corps organizations. Finally, there is a catchall category for military schools, including the Reserve Officer Training Corps (ROTC). Although there are no Coast Guard buckles included, no slight was intended. I'd like to include any you have available for the book's first revision.

The Four Military Buckle Types

The Four Military Buckle Types.
Top left: American Friction Buckle
Top right: British Two-piece Buckle
Bottom left: German Box Buckle
Bottom right: Russian Curved Buckle.

It came as a surprise to me to realize that the vast majority of **current** military buckles could be included in one of four types or styles:

1. American Friction
2. British Two-piece
3. German Box
4. Russian Curved.

The friction, two-piece, and box types were defined in the Introduction. The Russian curved type doesn't need much of a description. Basically, the buckle has an extreme curvature. You'll see examples of each of these four types throughout the book.

Usually, close allies of a country tend to have "cross-fertilization" of tactics, strategies, and equipment. Often there is a dominant allied partner, with more of its ideas and equipment being accepted than vice versa. Such is the case with buckles. For example, the former Soviet Union wielded enormous influence over other communist countries. As a result, you'll find curved military buckles in Cuba and in the former East Bloc countries.

Unfortunately, our analogy of cross-fertilization doesn't always work out. How can I explain, for example, a box buckle in use in Paraguay? Or that the two-piece type may be seen internationally with dress uniform buckles. I cannot. So, let's leave it that the four types of military buckles are a handy way of describing what we're looking at, and that the countries named – America, Britain, Germany, and Russia – **currently** use the type that is referenced to them to a great extent, but not exclusively.

U.S. Army

Different "Face" Widths of American Friction Buckles.
Top: U.S. Army Infantry, brass, c. 1958, uniform wear. Size 2.5" x 1.5". The Infantry insignia, crossed rifles, has been affixed to the buckle with a brass stud.
Price: $20 or less.
Bottom: U.S. Army, 1st Battalion, 2nd Infantry, brass, c. 1969, worn in the Republic of Vietnam with tropical worsted uniform. Size 1.75" x 1.5". The unit insignia has been engraved.
Price: $20 or less.

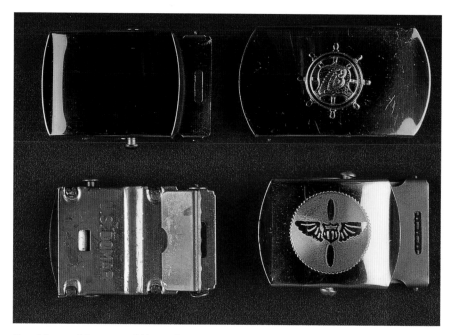

Four Views of American Military Friction Buckles.
Top left: Standard type, c. 2000.
Top right: Longer type with U.S. Army Transportation Corps insignia soldered to front, c. 1957.
Bottom left: Back of standard friction buckle, c. 1969.
Bottom right: Standard type with U.S. Army Air Corps insignia engraved into front, c. 1941.

U.S. Army 9ᵗʰ Infantry Friction Buckle, brass, c. 1972, uniform wear. Size 2.25" x 1.5". The unit insignia is die struck on a brass plate, which is then soldered to the buckle. **Price:** $21 to $40.

U.S. Army Officer's Mess Dress Buckle, brass, c. 1985, uniform wear with dress blues. Size 2" x 2". The U.S. Army's officer insignia is affixed to the buckle with two studs. **Price:** $21 to $40.

The Great War for Civilization, brass, c. 1920s, casual wear. Size 1.75" x 1.25". Probably privately purchased by a W.W.I veteran. The detail work on this buckle is outstanding. The center seal is a close copy of the front of the U.S. W.W.I Victory Medal. **Price:** $41 to $60.

U.S. Army 7th Cavalry, brass, c. 1976, casual wear. Size 2.5" in diameter. Commemorates Custer's unit. **Price:** $20 or less.

U.S. Army 49th Armor Division, brass with enamel, c. 1946, casual wear. Size 2.5" x 1". This style (curved brass facing soldered to front) has also been used to produce bracelets for the same unit. **Price:** $21 to $40.

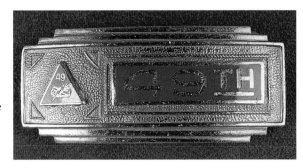

U.S. Army Combat Infantryman, pewter with color epoxy, c. 1998, casual wear. Size 3" x 2.25". The central design is the U.S. Army's coveted Combat Infantryman Badge. **Price:** $21 to $40.

Fort Eustis (Virginia), brass, c. 1972, casual wear. Size 2.5" x 2.5". Ft. Eustis is the location of the U.S. Army's Transportation Corps. **Price:** $20 or less.

Airborne, brass with silver wings, c. 1969, casual wear. Size 2.5" x 2.25". The insignia is the Airborne badge as used primarily by the U.S. Army and U.S. Air Force. It tells the world that the wearer is a "jumper!" **Price:** $20 or less.

Airborne, Death from Above, pewter, c. 1969, casual wear. Size 3.25" x 2.25". The Airborne insignia has been changed to incorporate a skull in the center. This design became common with Airborne and Special Forces units' unofficial cloth insignia in Vietnam. **Price:** $21 to $40.

Explosive Ordnance Disposal, brass, c. 1982, casual wear. Size 3.25" x 2.25". The insignia is the Master Explosive Ordnance Disposal badge. **Price:** $21 to $40.

AM General, Advanced Mobility, brass, c. 1989, casual wear. Size 3.5" x 2.25". Depicts the U.S. military's 2½ ton truck. **Price:** $20 or less.

U.S. Army Special Forces, brass, c. 1976, casual wear. Size 3.5" x 2.25". The motto, De Oppresso Liber, translates as "To Free the Oppressed." **Price:** $21 to $40.

32D AADCOM, Reenlist to Stay, brass, c. 1984, casual wear. Size 3.5" x 2.25". The wording urges soldiers to reenlist – an ongoing concern for the All Volunteer Army. **Price:** $21 to $40.

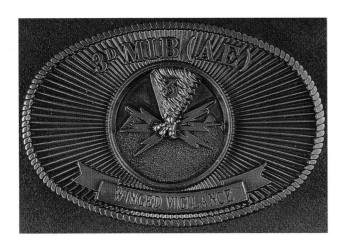

3rd MIB (AE), brass, c. 1988, casual wear. Size 3.5" x 2.25". The unit is the 3rd Military Intelligence Battalion, U.S. Army. **Price:** $21 to $40.

MLRS, brass, c. 1985, casual wear. Size 3.5" x 2.25". "MLRS" stands for "Multiple Launch Rocket System" **Price:** $21 to $40.

U.S. Army MASH, brass with olive drab paint, c. 1985, casual wear. Size 2.5" x 1.25". The buckle is shaped as a U.S. military identification tag and was produced in conjunction with the TV show of the same name. **Price:** $21 to $40.

Front of Authentic versus Reproduction 1874 U.S. Army Officer's Buckle.
Top: Authentic 1874 U.S. Army Officer's pattern, worn 1874-1920. Die-struck brass with silvered details. Size of face: 2.75" x 2". **Price:** $81 to $100.
Bottom: Reproduction of 1874 pattern buckle. Produced c. 1980. Cast base metal. Size of face: 2.75" x 2". **Price:** $10 or less.

Back of Authentic versus Reproduction 1874 U.S. Army Officer's Buckle.
Top: Authentic 1874 U.S. Army Officer's pattern. The die striking is clearly visible in the center of the buckle. The catch (on the left) is quite large, almost a full 2".
Bottom: Reproduction of 1874 pattern buckle. The casting method produced a flat back with no detail. The catch (on the left) consists of a simple, small cast hook. The wire attachment (on the right) is considerably different from the authentic buckle's attachment.

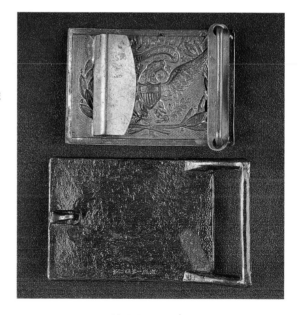

Reproduction U.S. Military Buckles, all of brass. All are extremely high quality reproductions made by Hanover Brass Foundry, Mechanicsville, Virginia. Owner Gary Williams produces buckles for reenactors, not for those few deceptive dealers. But, the lesson is clear: know your buckles and whom you're buying from. **Price each:** $20 or less.

Top left: Musician's two-piece belt plate, originally made c. 1860.
Top right: Virginia two-piece belt plate, originally made c. 1840
Bottom left: Early Militia two-piece belt plate, originally made c. 1850
Bottom right: Virginia belt plate, originally made c. 1850.

Reproduction Militia Artillery Belt Plate, brass, originally made c. 1810. Size 2.5" x 2.5". Another excellent reproduction by Gary Williams. **Price:** $20 or less.

Commemorative Civil War Buckle, pewter with enamel Confederate battle flag, c. 1999, casual wear. Size 4" x 3". Part of a set, one for each Southern State. **Price:** $20 or less.

Foreign Armies

Republic of Vietnam Military Officer Academy, Dalat, brass with enamel, c. 1960s, uniform wear. Size 3.5" x 3". The center design is a dragon with sword coiled around a map of South Vietnam. **Price:** $121 to $140.

Republic of Vietnam Army Officer, brass, c. 1969, uniform wear. Size 2.25" x 2". The catch (that goes on the left) is missing. **Price:** $61 to $80.

North Vietnamese Army, two-piece brass with raised star, c. 1968, uniform wear. Size 1.5" x 1.75". This is a highly prized "bring back" of veterans of the Vietnam War. **Price:** $81 to $100.

North Vietnamese Army, two-piece brass with incised star, c. 1968, uniform wear. Size 2.25" x 2". Attached to a rubber belt made to look like leather. **Price:** $81 to $100.

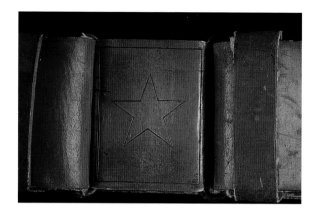

North Vietnamese Army, two-piece steel with incised star, c. 1968, uniform wear. Size 2.75" x 2.5". Attached to a cloth pistol belt. Probably manufactured in the People's Republic of China. **Price:** $81 to $100.

People's Republic of China Armed Forces, two-piece steel with incised star with a Chinese ideogram in the center, c. 1997, uniform wear. Size 2.75" x 2.5". Attached to a fiber belt made to look like leather. Notice the strong similarity to the North Vietnamese Army buckle in the previous photo. **Price:** $41 to $60.

Philippine Army, chrome, c. 1951, uniform wear. Size 2.25" x 1.5". Somewhat worn and "dinged up." **Price:** $10 or less.

Italian Army, tentative identification, steel friction buckle, c. 1980s, uniform wear. Size 2.5" x 1.75". **Price:** $20 or less.

Laos Army, brass friction buckle, c. 1988, uniform wear. Size 2.5" x 1.5". **Price:** $20 or less.

Singapore Army, chrome, c. 1982, uniform wear. Size 2.25" x 1.5". **Price:** $20 or less.

Two Republic of Korea Army (ROKA) buckles, both brass, c. 1990s, uniform wear. **Price each:** $20 or less.
Left: The 9th Special Forces Brigade, ROKA. Size 2.25" x 1.25".
Right: Airborne unit, Master Parachutist qualification. Size 2" x 1.25".

Imperial Russian Army, brass curved buckle, c. 1912, uniform wear. Size 3.25" x 2.25". Due to the curvature of most Russian buckles, they are difficult to photograph. **Price:** $81 to $100.

71

Front of Authentic versus Reproduction Soviet Army Buckles.
Top: Authentic Soviet Army buckle, die-struck curved brass, c. 1986, uniform wear. Size 3" x 2". **Price:** $10 or less.
Bottom: Reproduction Soviet Army buckle, die-struck brass, no curve, produced c. 1994, unknown wear. Size 3" x 2". **Price:** $10 or less. Another mystery: why reproduce a relatively common buckle and charge the same price? The only answer heard so far is that the reproduction can be worn on American-style belts.

Back of Authentic versus Reproduction Soviet Army Buckles.
Top: Authentic Soviet Army buckle, with wide hook (on the right).
Bottom: Reproduction Soviet Army buckle, with small hook (on the right).

Comparison of Front of Cuban versus Soviet Army Buckles. The similarities are *not* very apparent.
Top: Cuban Army, curved steel, c. 1988, uniform wear. Size 3" x 2". **Price:** $61 to $80.
Bottom: Soviet Army, curved brass, c. 1987, uniform wear. Size 3" x 2". **Price:** $10 or less.

Comparison of Back of Cuban versus Soviet Army. Buckles. The similarities are now *very* apparent. **Top:** Cuban Army. **Bottom:** Soviet Army.

Close up of Front of Cuban Buckle. Curved style is definitely of Russian origin. The buckle was attached to a well-worn field belt of impregnated brown canvas.

73

Mongolian Army, curved brass, c. 1942, uniform wear. Size 1.5" x 2". **Price:** $61 to $80.

Soviet Army General's Buckle, curved brass, c. 1967, uniform wear. Size 2.25" x 2.25". Attached to a brown leather "Sam Browne" belt of high-quality construction. **Price:** $121 to $140.

Ukrainian Army, curved brass, c. 1999, uniform wear. Size 3" x 2". **Price:** $61 to $80.

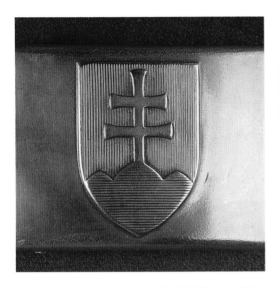

Slovenian Army, tentative identification, brass box buckle, c. 1998, uniform wear. Size 2.5" x 2". **Price:** $61 to $80.

Slovenian Army, tentative identification, chrome two-piece with colored enamel, c. 1999, uniform wear. Size 1.75" x 1.25". **Price:** $41 to $60.

Yugoslavian National Army, brass friction buckle, c. 1988, uniform wear. Size 1.75" x 1.25". **Price:** $21 to $40.

Yugoslavian National Army Officer' Dress Buckle, East Bloc, two-piece brass, c. 1984, uniform wear. Size 3" x 2". **Price:** $61 to $80.

Yugoslavian Army Officer's Dress Buckle, Current, brass buckle with color enamel, c. 1999, uniform wear. Size 2" x 2.5". **Price:** $41 to $60.

Czechoslovakian Army General's Dress Buckle, two-piece brass, c. 1984, uniform wear. Attached to a brocade belt. Size 1.75" x 1.25". **Price:** $81 to $100.

Hungarian Army General's Dress Buckle, brass, c. 1982, uniform wear. Attached to a brocade belt. Size 3" x 2". **Price:** $81 to $100.

Rumanian Army General's Dress Buckle, brass, c. 1986, uniform wear. Attached to a brocade belt. Size 2" in diameter. **Price:** $81 to $100.

German Army (Heer) Enlisted, aluminum with traces of gray paint, c. 1942, uniform wear. Average condition. Size 2.5" x 1.75". **Price:** $61 to $80.

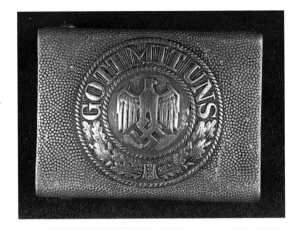

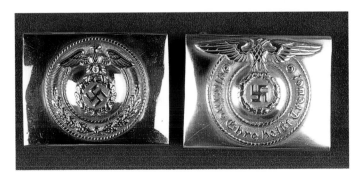

Two Reproduction German Third Reich buckles.
Left: Stormabteilung (SA) buckle in chrome. Size 2.5" x 1.75".
Price: $20 or less.
Right: Schutzstaffel (SS) buckle in aluminum. Size 2.5 x 1.75".
Probably the single most reproduced buckle in the world! **Price:** $20 or less.

Jungsturm (Youth Platoon) of the Reichsbanner Organization, brass with chrome center, c. 1930, uniform wear. Authentic buckle of an *anti-Nazi* group. Size 2.5" x 1.75". **Price:** $61 to $80.

Prussian Army Telegraph Troops, painted steel in below average condition, c. W.W.I, uniform wear. Clips on left and right ends held a reel of signal wire. Size 4.25" x 1.75". **Price:** $61 to $80.

Two East German (DDR) Buckles, both steel, c. 1980s, uniform wear. Commonly available. **Price each:** $10 or less.

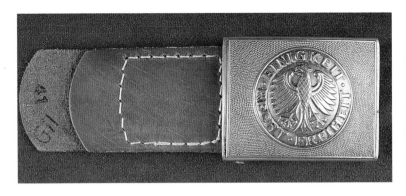

Current German Army, steel box buckle with leather tab (lederwiderhalt) attached, c. 1991, uniform wear. Size 2.75" x 2". **Price:** $20 or less.

Spanish Army, tentative identification, brass, c. 1930s, uniform wear. Size 2.5" x 3.25". **Price:** $41 to $60.

Spanish Army, chrome, c. 1980s, uniform wear. Size 2" x 1.5". **Price:** $20 or less.

Saudi Arabia Armed Forces, matte brass, c. 1996, uniform wear. Made in the good ol' USA! Size 1.75" x 1.5". **Price:** $10 or less.

Trinidad and Tobago Regiment, brass two-piece with chrome, age unknown, uniform wear. Size 4.5" x 2.75". **Price:** $41 to $60.

Republic of Paraguay, brass box buckle, age unknown, uniform wear. Size 2.5" x 1.75". Although this is a box buckle the post pin and catch are on the opposite sides when compared to German box buckles. **Price:** $21 to $40.

Bolivian Army, tentative identification, brass, c. 1980s, uniform wear. Size 1.75" x 1.5". **Price:** $20 or less.

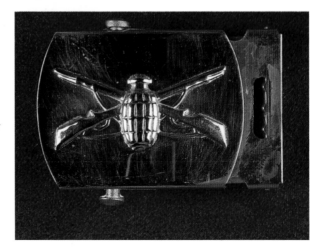

London Scottish Volunteers (England), two-piece chrome, age unknown, uniform wear. Size 3.75" x 1.75". The thistles on either side of the center section are very detailed. **Price:** $101 to $120.

Four British General Service Pattern Buckles, all are two-piece brass (although more recent models have appeared in chrome). Dates of usage vary, but notice the subtle difference in the shape and size of the belt keeper loops and the crowns in the center designs. All are uniform wear. Size approximately 3.5" x 2.5". **Price each:** $41 to $60.

Royal Highland Light Infantry of Canada (The 13th), brass, c. 1950s, uniform wear. Size 4" x 2.25". **Price:** $21 to $40.

82

Two Reproduction British Buckles, both for the 24th Foot of the 2nd Warwickshire Regiment, current production. **Price each:** $10 or less.
Top: Officer, brass and aluminum. Size 4" x 2".
Bottom: Other ranks (enlisted), brass. Size 3.75" x 2". Compare either of these poor quality copies to the authentic, finely crafted British buckles in this section.

Two British Guards Regiment Buckles, both brass, c. 1960s, uniform wear. Size 3.5" x 2.5". **Price each:** $41 to $60.
Top: Irish Guards, in excellent condition.
Bottom: Welsh Guards, in average condition with loss of detail due to polishing.

Two Canadian Buckles, uniform wear. **Price each:** $20 or less.
Top: Royal Canadian Electrical and Mechanical Engineers, brass with chrome horse and globe, age unknown. Size 3.5" x 2.5".
Bottom: Canadian Armed Forces, brass, current issue. Size 3" x 2.5".

Top: Royal Montreal Regiment (The 14th), brass, age unknown, uniform
wear. Size 3.75" x 2.75". **Price:** $20 or less.
Bottom: Royal Canadian Ordnance Corps, brass, age unknown,
uniform wear. Size 3.75" x 2.75". **Price:** $20 or less.

Top left: Royal Canadian Army Medical Corps, brass, age unknown, uniform wear.
Size 3.75" x 2.75". **Price:** $20 or less.
Top right: Queen's Own Cameron Highlanders of Canada, brass, age unknown,
uniform wear. Size 4" x 2.25". **Price:** $20 or less.
Bottom left: Princess Patricia's Canadian Light Infantry, chrome (or perhaps brass
plating with most worn off), age unknown, uniform wear. Size 4" x 2.25". **Price:** $20
or less.
Bottom right: Lord Strathconas Horse (Royal Canadian), brass, age unknown,
uniform wear. Size 3.75" x 2.75". **Price:** $20 or less.

Rhodesian Army, brass, c. 1960s, uniform wear. Size 4" x 2.25". The same design is sometimes encountered in chrome. **Price:** $41 to $60.

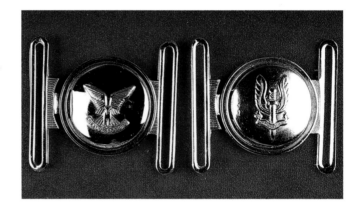

Left: Selous Scouts, Rhodesia, chrome, age unknown, uniform wear. Size 3" x 2.75". **Price:** $81 to $100.
Right: Rhodesian Special Air Service, chrome, age unknown, uniform wear. Size 3" x 2.75". **Price:** $81 to $100.

Tanzania Armed Forces, brass, c. 1992, uniform wear. Size 4" x 2.5". **Price:** $41 to $60.

Top: 4th Artillery Regiment, Republic of South Africa, chrome with pewter and red plastic, c. 1994, uniform wear. Size 5" x 2.75". **Price:** $21 to $40.
Bottom: 10th Artillery Brigade, Republic of South Africa, chrome with pewter and red plastic, c. 1997, uniform wear. Size 5" x 2.75". **Price:** $21 to $40.

Special Service Battalion, Republic of South Africa, brass, c. 1990, uniform wear. The center of the buckle features a protea plant, which is native to South Africa. Size 3.25" x 2.5". **Price:** $41 to $60.

Top: Special Forces, Transkei Defense Force, chrome with brass, c. 1997, uniform wear. Size 3.25" x 2.5". **Price:** $21 to $40.
Bottom: Rhodesian Armored Car Regiment, chrome, c. 1976, uniform wear. Size 3.25" x 2.5". **Price:** $61 to $80.

Top: Bophuthatswana Defense Force, chrome with brass, c. 1995, uniform wear. Size 3" x 2.75". **Price:** $21 to $40.
Bottom: Kwazulu Armed Forces, tentative identification, chrome with brass, c. 1998, uniform wear. Note that the dark spot at bottom of buckle is a reflection. Size 3" x 2.75". **Price:** $21 to $40.

Mexican Armed Forces Buckles.
Top left: Navy, brass, c. 2000, uniform wear. Size 2.5" x 1.5". **Price:** $20 or less.
Top right: Army, brass friction buckle, c. 2000, uniform wear. Size 2" x 1.25". **Price:** $20 or less.
Bottom: Navy, brass, c. 2000, reportedly only worn by females in naval service, uniform wear. Size 2.5" x 1.5". **Price:** $20 or less.

U.S. Navy

U. S. Navy Officer, 1905 Pattern, brass, c. 1910, uniform wear. The keeper (on the right) does not appear to be original to the buckle. Size 3" x 2". **Price:** $101 to $120.

Underwater Demolition Team (UDT), Sea, Air, Land (SEAL), brass, c. 1994, casual wear. Size 3.75" x 2.5". **Price:** $21 to $40.

U.S. Navy, Enlisted, pewter, c. 1987, casual wear. Size 2.5" x 2". **Price:** $20 or less.

U. S. Navy, Enlisted, brass friction buckle with chrome, c. 1984, uniform wear. Size 2" x 1.5". **Price:** $20 or less.

U. S. Navy, Philippines, steel, c. 1946, uniform wear. Commemorates a sailor's service at Subic Bay, just after the end of W.W.II. Size 3.25" x 2.5". **Price:** $61 to $80.

U.S. Navy Submarine Service, pewter with enamel, c. 1980, casual wear. Size 3.25" x 2". **Price:** $20 or less.

USS Dwight D. Eisenhower, brass friction buckle, c. 1986, uniform wear. Size 2" x 1.5". **Price:** $20 or less.

Top: Naval Aviator Wings, brass friction buckle, c. 2000, uniform wear. Size 3" x 1.5". **Price:** $20 or less.
Middle: USS Sellers, DDG 11, chrome friction buckle with enamel, c. 1984, uniform wear. Size 2.5" x 1.5". **Price:** $20 or less.
Bottom: USS New York City, SSN 696, brass friction buckle, c. 2000, uniform wear. The center design is of the Submarine Service's qualification badge. Size 3" x 1.5". **Price:** $20 or less.

Top: USS John F. Kennedy, CV-67, chrome friction buckle, c. 1989, uniform wear. Size 2.5" x 1.5". **Price:** $20 or less.
Middle: Naval Flight Officer (USN), chrome friction buckle with gilt detailing, age unknown, uniform wear. Size 3" x 1.5". **Price:** $21 to $40.
Bottom: USS Ainsworth, FF-1090, chrome friction buckle, c. 1984, uniform wear. Size 3" x 1.5". **Price:** $20 or less.

USS Harry E. Yarnell, CG-17, brass, c. 1998, uniform wear. Size 3" x 1.5". **Price:** $20 or less.

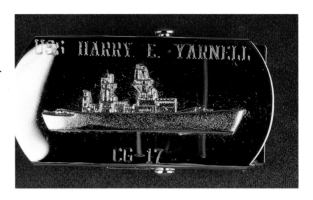

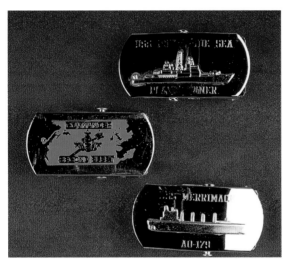

Top: USS Philippine Sea, Plank Owner, brass friction buckle, c. 2000, uniform wear. A "plank owner" is a crewmember on a ship's maiden voyage. Size 3" x 1.5". **Price:** $21 to $40.
Middle: Commander, Second Fleet (USN), chrome friction buckle with enamel, age unknown, uniform wear. Size 3" x 1.5". **Price:** $21 to $40.
Bottom: USS Merrimack, AD-179, brass friction buckle, c. 2000, uniform wear. Size 3" x 1.5". **Price:** $20 or less.

F-14 Tomcat, brass with gilt detailing, c. 1996, uniform wear. Size 3.5" x 2.5". **Price:** $20 or less.

Foreign Navies

Front of Authentic versus Reproduction Soviet Navy Buckles.
Top: Authentic Soviet Navy, die-struck curved brass, c. 1984, uniform wear. Size 3" x 2". **Price:** $20 or less.
Bottom: Reproduction Soviet Navy buckle, die-struck brass, no curve, produced c. 1994, unknown wear. Size 3" x 2". **Price:** $10 or less.

Back of Authentic versus Reproduction Soviet Navy Buckles.
Top: Authentic Soviet Navy buckle, with wide hook (on the right).
Bottom: Reproduction Soviet Navy buckle, with small hook (on the right).

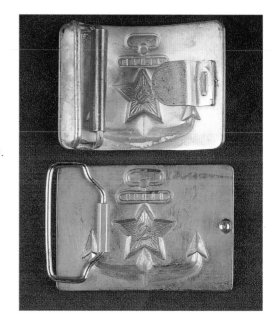

Soviet Merchant Navy, tentative identification, die-struck curved brass, c. 1982, uniform wear. Size 3" x 2". **Price:** $21 to $40.

Comparison of Soviet Navy and Army Dress Buckles. Both are the same size and shape. Only the center design is different.
Left: Navy, brass, c. 1986, uniform wear. Center design is an anchor with a star at the top. Size 1.5" x 2". **Price:** $41 to $60.
Right: Army, brass, c. 1982, uniform wear. Center design is a hammer and sickle inside of a star. Size 1.5" x 2". **Price:** $21 to $40.

Soviet Navy Dress Buckle, Junior Officer, tentative identification, brass, c. 1985, uniform wear. Size 1.5" in diameter. **Price:** $41 to $60.

93

British Navy, two-piece brass, age unknown, uniform wear. The motto, "Si vis pacem, para bellum," translates as "If you want peace, prepare for war." Size 3.75" x 2.25". **Price:** $61 to $80.

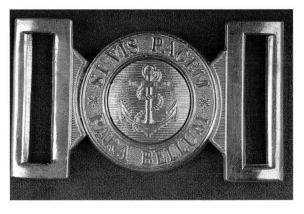

French Navy, curved brass, c. 1985, uniform wear. Size 2" x 2". **Price:** $21 to $40.

German Navy, two-piece aluminum, c. 1940s, uniform wear. Reportedly worn by naval administrative officers. Size 3" x 2.5". **Price:** $81 to $100.

Yugoslavian Navy, chrome with enamel, c. 1980, uniform wear. Size 1.75" x 1.25". **Price:** $20 or less.

Japanese Navy, officer, two-piece brass, c. W.W.II, uniform wear. Size 3.5" x 2". **Price:** $101 to $120.

Left: Malaysian Army, brass friction buckle, c. 1992, uniform wear. Size 1.75" x 1.5". **Price:** $20 or less.
Right: Malaysian Navy, brass friction buckle, c. 1992, uniform wear. Size 1.75" x 1.5". **Price:** $20 or less.

Thailand Navy, Officer, two-piece brass, c. 1980, uniform wear. Size 3" x 2.5". **Price:** $60 to $80.

U.S. Air Force and Foreign Air Forces

Two U.S. Air Force Buckles.
Top: Chrome with gilt detailing, age unknown, casual wear. Size 3.5" x 2.5".
Price: $21 to $40.
Bottom: Pewter, c. 1985, casual wear. Size 2.25" x 1.5". **Price:** $20 or less.

Royal Canadian Air Force, brass friction buckle with enamel, c. 1990, uniform wear. Size 1.75" x 1.5". **Price:** $20 or less.

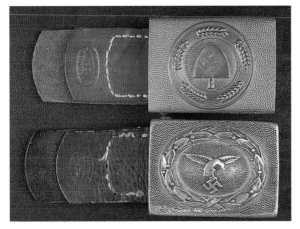

Two German Third Reich Buckles, both are the same size and shape. Only the design is different. Both have the leather tab attached.
Top: Reichsarbeitsdienst (National Labor Service), Enlisted, aluminum, c. W.W.II, uniform wear. Center design is a swastika superimposed on a spade. Size 2.5" x 1.75". **Price:** $101 to $120.
Bottom: Air Force (Luftwaffe), Enlisted, aluminum, c. W.W.II, uniform wear. Center design is an eagle (with tail down) above a swastika. Size 2.5" x 1.75". **Price:** $101 to $120.

Negev Air Base (Israel), Constructors, brass, c. 1979, unknown wear. Size 3" x 2". **Price:** $20 or less.

Yugoslavian Air Force, chrome friction buckle with enamel, c. 1986, uniform wear. Size 1.75" x 1.5". **Price:** $20 or less.

Spanish Air Force, curved brass, age unknown, uniform wear. Size 3" x 2". **Price:** $41 to $60.

U.S. Marine Corps

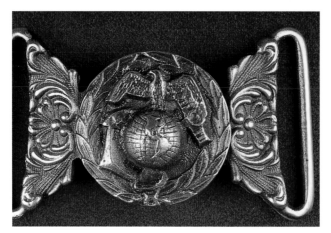

U.S. Marine Corps, reproduction, two-piece brass, manufactured c. 1998, casual wear. Produced by Hanover Brass Foundry. Size 3" x 1.75". **Price:** $20 or less.

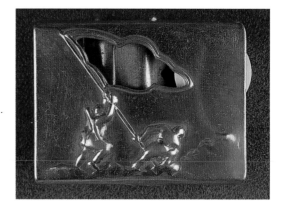

Raising the Flag on Iwo Jima, brass friction buckle, age unknown, casual wear. This is a curious rendition of this famous event, with only *two* Marines. Size 1.75" x 1.5". **Price:** $21 to $40.

Delta, 4th Recon, USMC, bronze, c. 1988, casual wear. Force Recon is the Marine Corps' version of special forces. Size 4" x 2.25". **Price:** $21 to $40.

U.S. Marine Corps, brass friction buckle, age unknown, casual wear. Size 2.75" x 1.5". **Price:** $21 to $40.

U.S. Marine Corps, gold-plate and silver plate with enamel, c. 1998, casual wear. Size 3.75" x 2.75". **Price:** $60 to $80.

U.S. Marines, Fourth Division, brass, c. 1993, casual wear. The Fourth is the Reserve Division. Size 3.5" x 2.25". **Price:** $21 to $40.

U.S. Marine Corps Dress Uniform Buckles, brass. The top buckle has a special "no polish" protective coating. The bottom buckle shows the effects of tarnish, and looks "salty" (as Marines would say, although they'd never wear a buckle looking like this on a uniform!) Size 3" x 2". **Price each:** $21 to $40.

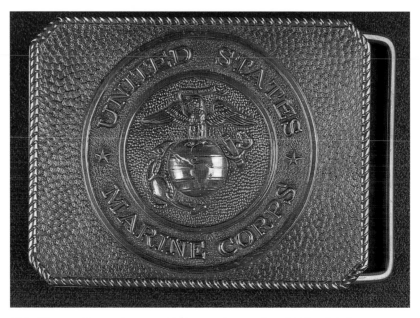

U.S. Marine Corps, brass, c. 1969, casual wear. Size 2.75" x 2.25". **Price:** $21 to $40.

USMC, brass, c. 1976, casual wear. Jokesters suggest that "USMC" really stands for "Uncle Sam's Misguided Children." Size 1.75" x 1.25". **Price:** $20 or less.

U.S. Marine Corps, brass, c. 1988, casual wear. Size 2.5" in diameter. **Price:** $21 to $40.

U.S. Marine Corps, brass, c. 1980, casual wear. Size 2.75" x 2.25". **Price:** $21 to $40.

Foreign Marine Corps

British Royal Marines, brass, c. W.W.II, uniform wear. It is attached to a non-issue nylon belt. There is some loss of detail due to polishing. Size 3.25" x 2.25". **Price:** $61 to $80.

Republic of Korea (ROK) Marine Corps.
Top: ROK Force Recon, brass friction buckle, c. 1986, unknown wear. Size 2.75" x 1.5". **Price:** $21 to $40.
Bottom left: Standard U.S. military friction buckle, c. 1990, uniform wear. Size 2" x 1.5". **Price:** $5 or less.
Bottom right: ROK Marine Corps, brass friction buckle, c. 1989, unknown wear. The similarity of the ROK Marine Corps seal to the U.S. Marine Corps seal indicates their close ties. Size 2" x 1.5". **Price:** $21 to $40.

Other Military Organizations

Grand Army of the Republic (GAR), brass, c. 1910, uniform wear. The GAR, founded in 1866, was the preeminent organization of Union veterans of the American Civil War. There are numerous versions of this buckle, all fairly roughly cast. Size 2.75" x 2". **Price:** $101 to $120.

West Point, U.S.M.A., pewter, c. 1980, casual wear. Size 3.5" x 2.5". **Price:** $21 to $40.

U.S.M.A. Buckles, both brass, c. 1960s, uniform wear. Shown both without (top) and with (bottom) the belt keeper. Size 3" x 2". **Price:** $21 to $40.

Two Military School Buckles.
Top: United States Military Academy (U.S.M.A.), brass, c. 1956, uniform wear. Shown with belt keeper. Size 3.75" x 2". **Price:** $21 to $40.
Bottom: Reserve Officer Training Corps (ROTC), Virginia Polytechnic Institute and State University, brass, c. 1976, uniform wear. Shown without belt keeper. Size 3" x 2". **Price:** $21 to $40.

Additional Military School Buckles.
Top left: Staunton (Virginia), Cadet, chrome, c. 1984, uniform wear. Size 3" x 2". **Price:** $21 to $40.
Top right: Fork Union (Virginia), brass, c. 1994, uniform wear. Size 3" x 1.75". **Price:** $21 to $40.
Bottom left: Massanutten (Virginia), chrome, c. 1992, uniform wear. Size 2.75" x 1.75". **Price:** $21 to $40.
Bottom right: Virginia Polytechnic Institute and State University (ROTC), chrome and brass, age unknown, uniform wear. Size 2.5" x 2". **Price:** $21 to $40.

Harrisburg Academy, pewter, age unknown, uniform wear. Size 2" in diameter. **Price:** $20 or less.

A Common Naval Heritage.
Left: U.S. Coast Guard Academy, chrome, c. 1970, uniform wear. Size 3" x 2.25".
Price: $41 to $60.
Right: U.S. Naval Academy, chrome, c. 1964, uniform wear. Size 3" x 2.25". **Price:** $41 to $60.

Top: Remember the Alamo, brass, c. 1975, casual wear. Size 3.5" x 2".
Price: $20 or less.
Bottom: Vietnam Remembered, chrome with gilt, c. 1990, casual wear. Size 3.5" x 2". **Price:** $21 to $40.

105

CCC (U.S. Civilian Conservation Corps), brass, c. 1938, unknown wear. The CCC, founded in 1933, initially had its camps administered by the U.S. Army. Thus, formed along military lines, it was unofficially known as "the Tree Army." Size 2.75" x 2". **Price:** $41 to $60.

U.S. CCC (U.S. Civilian Conservation Corps), chrome with enamel, c. 1936, unknown wear. Size 1.25" x 1.5". **Price:** $20 or less.

Israeli Gadna, brass, c. 1984, uniform wear. The Gadna is Israel's pre-military training organization. Attached to a tan canvas belt. Size 3" x 2". **Price:** $20 or less.

Mexican Pre-military Organization, tentative identification, chrome, c. 1999, unknown wear. Size 3.5" x 2.25". **Price:** $20 or less.

Youth Group Buckles

Overview

There are literally thousands of youth groups around the world. But, few of them wear distinctive uniforms that include a specially designed belt buckle. Since this book is only interested in presenting men's, and young men's, buckles, the focus narrows even more. The largest youth group that uses specially designed buckles is the world's Scouting movement. The predominant style of Scouting buckle is a British two-piece type, since the founder of the movement, Lord Baden-Powell, was British. However, there are many other types in use as well. There are, for example, large numbers of the American friction buckles used, too.

The intent of this chapter was to include all of the world's male youth organizations' buckles. But, with one exception, a British Boys' Brigade buckle, only Scouting movement buckles were found. Are there other types out there? If so, please let me know and they'll be included in a future edition of this book.

Now, on to the buckles. The U.S. examples are shown first, followed by the foreign buckles. Note that the identification of the foreign buckles, in particular, is often tentative since many use a Scouting symbol, the fleur-de-lis, alone or with a few letters that stand for the organization's full name.

U.S. Scouting Buckles

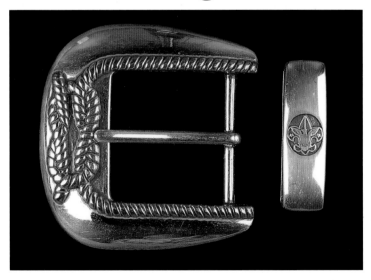

Boy Scouts of America (BSA), chrome with brass western style buckle, c. 2000, casual wear. Size 2.5 x 2.5". Comes with one belt keeper. **Price:** $20 or less.

Additional BSA Buckles.
Top left: National Law Enforcement Explorer Conference, brass, age unknown, casual wear. Size 2.5" in diameter. **Price:** $10 or less.
Top right: BSA (Eagle Scout), brass, c. 2000, unknown wear. Size 2.5" x 2". **Price:** $10 or less.
Bottom left: Wonderful World of Scouting, brass, c. 1990, unknown wear. Size 3" x 2". **Price:** $10 or less.
Bottom right: Order of the Arrow, Boy Scouts of America, pewter with enamel, c. 2000, uniform wear. Size 2.5" in diameter. **Price:** $20 or less.

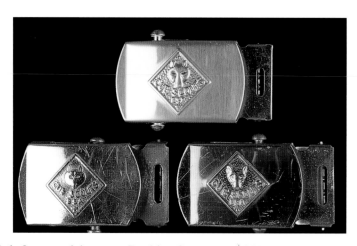

Three Cub Scouts of America Buckles Spanning 46 Years.
Top: Current model (c. 2000), brass friction type, uniform wear. Size 1.75" x 1". **Price:** $5 or less.
Bottom left: Author's buckle (c. 1954), brass friction type, uniform wear. Size 1.75" x 1". **Price:** $5 or less.
Bottom right: Author's son's buckle (c. 1975), brass friction type, uniform wear. Size 1.75" x 1" **Price:** $5 or less.
 You'd need excellent vision to notice any differences in the three buckles. Hint: look closely at the cubs' ears and muzzles.

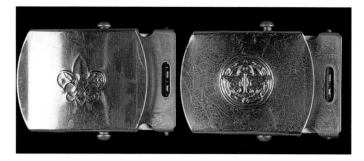

Left: Boy Scouts of America, brass friction buckle, c. 1963, uniform wear. Size 2" x 1.5". **Price:** $5 or less.
Right: Explorer Scout, brass friction buckle, c. 1956, uniform wear. Size 2" x 1.5". **Price:** $20 or less.

Left: Webelos, brass friction buckle, c. 2000, uniform wear. Size 1.75" x 1.25". **Price:** $5 or less.
Right: Tiger Cubs BSA, brass friction buckle, c. 2000, uniform wear. Size 1.75" x 1.25". **Price:** $5 or less.

The Negative Effects of Wear, both buckles from the Mason-Dixon Council, brass over base metal, c. 1978, casual wear. Size 2" in diameter.
Left: Unworn buckle. **Price:** $5 or less.
Right: Worn out buckle! **Price:** $1 or less.

This Space for Rent! Leather over metal frame, c. 1994, casual wear. Size 3.5" x 2.5". Sample buckle produced for a dealer display. **Price:** $20 or less.

Top left: San Mateo County Council (BSA), brass over base metal, c. 1995, casual wear. Size 2" x 2". **Price:** $5 or less.
Top right: Boy Scouts of America, Eagle Scout, pewter with epoxy, c. 2000, unknown wear. Size 2.75" x 2.5". **Price:** $20 or less.
Bottom: Scout emblem on generic buckle, c. 2000, casual wear. Size 2.5" x 2". **Price:** $5 or less.

Top left: National Scout Jamboree, Virginia, brass, 1981, casual wear. Size 2.75" x 2". **Price:** $20 or less.

Top right: National Jamboree, Washington, D.C., 1937, pewter, c. 1998, casual wear. One of a *recent* series of Jamboree buckles. Size 3" x 2". **Price:** $20 or less.

Bottom left: Boy Scouts of America (with American flag in background), pewter with enamel, c. 1999, unknown wear. Size 2.5" x 2". **Price:** $20 or less.

Bottom right: Philmont Scout Ranch (New Mexico), brass, c. 1965, uniform wear. Size 3" x 1.75". **Price:** $20 or less.

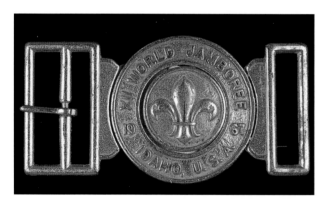

12ᵗʰ World Jamboree, Idaho, USA, two-piece brass, c. 1967, uniform wear. Size 3.25" x 1.5". **Price:** $20 or less.

Boy Scouts of America, Be Prepared, two-piece brass, c. 1977, uniform wear. Size 2" x 1.5". **Price:** $20 or less.

Foreign Youth Group Buckles

Boy Scouts of Thailand, two-piece brass, c. 1977, uniform wear. Size 4" x 2.25". **Price:** $21 to $40.

The Boy's Brigade (England), two-piece brass, unknown date, uniform wear. This organization is comparable in purpose to the Boy Scouts. Size 3" x 2". **Price:** $20 or less.

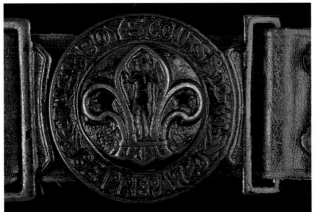

British Boy Scout Leader, tentative identification, two-piece blackened metal, age unknown, uniform wear. Size 3" x 1.75". **Price:** $10 or less.

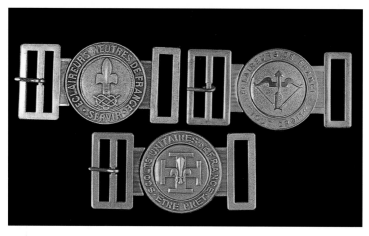

French Scout Buckles
Top left: Eclaireurs Neutres de France, two-piece base metal, c. 1997, uniform wear. Size 2.5" x 1.5". **Price:** $20 or less.
Top right: Eclaireurs de France, two-piece brass, c. 1988, uniform wear. Size 2.5" x 1.5". **Price:** $20 or less.
Bottom: Scouts Unitaires de France, two-piece brass, c. 1998, casual wear. Size 2.5" x 2". **Price:** $20 or less.

Mexican Scout Buckles.
Top left: Brass friction buckle, c. 1999, uniform wear. Size 2" x 1.25". **Price:** $5 or less.
Top right: Brass friction buckle, c. 1999, uniform wear. Size 2" x 1.25". **Price:** $5 or less.
Bottom left: Two-piece brass, c. 2000, uniform wear. Size 3.25" x 2". **Price:** $20 or less.
Bottom right: Two-piece brass with enamel, c. 2000, uniform wear. Size 2.25" x 1". **Price:** $5 or less.

Scouts Canada, two-piece chrome, c. 1996, uniform wear. Attached to a brown leather belt. Size 3.5" x 1.75". **Price:** $20 or less.

113

Top left: British Wolf Cubs, two-piece chrome, age unknown, uniform wear. Size 2.75" x 1.5". **Price:** $5 or less.

Top right: Netherlands Scouts, tentative identification, two-piece brass, c. 1996, uniform wear. Size 3.25" x 2". **Price:** $5 or less.

Bottom left: Verbond der Katholieke Scouts (German Catholic Scouts), tentative identification, two-piece chrome, age unknown, uniform wear. Size 3" x 1.75". **Price:** $10 or less.

Bottom right: British Boy Scouts, tentative identification, two-piece chrome, c. 1998, uniform wear. Size 3" x 1.5". **Price:** $5 or less.

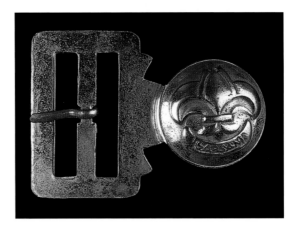

Republic of Vietnam Boy Scouts, two-piece chrome (one half of buckle missing), c. 1966, uniform wear. The motto, Sap San, translates to "Be Prepared." Estimated size if complete buckle present: 3" x 1.5". **Price:** $20 or less.

Top left: Switzerland Boy Scouts, tentative identification, two-piece brass, c. 1988, uniform wear. Size 3.25" x 1.75". **Price:** $20 or less.

Top right: Spanish Catholic Scouts, tentative identification, two-piece brass, c. 1991, uniform wear. Size 3.25" x 1.75". **Price:** $20 or less.

Bottom left: Czech Boy Scouts, two-piece brass, age unknown, uniform wear. Size 3" x 1.75". **Price:** $20 or less.

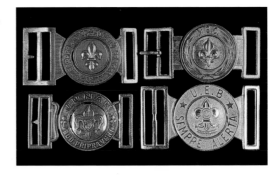

Bottom right: Brazil Boy Scouts, two-piece brass, c. 1996, uniform wear. Size 3.25" x 2". **Price:** $20 or less.

Malaysia Boy Scouts, two-piece chrome, c. 1989, uniform wear. Size 3" x 1.5". **Price:** $10 or less.

Allzeit Bereit (Austrian Boy Scouts), tentative identification, two-piece chrome, c. 1989, uniform wear. Attached to a black leather belt. Size 3.5" x 1.75". **Price:** $20 or less.

German Scouts, tentative identification, two-piece chrome, age unknown, uniform wear. Attached to a brown leather belt. Size 3.5" x 1.75". **Price:** $20 or less.

Singapore Scouts, two-piece chrome, c. 1968, uniform wear. Attached to a brown leather belt. Size 3" x 1.75". **Price:** $20 or less.

Pakistan Scouts, two-piece brass, age unknown, uniform wear. Attached to a khaki belt. Size 3.25" x 1.75". **Price:** $20 or less.

Kuwait Boy Scouts, two-piece
brass, c. 1979, uniform wear. Size
3.5" x 1.75". **Price:** $21 to $40.

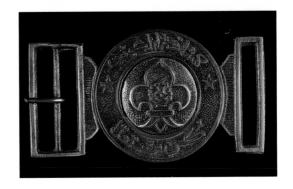

Greek Scouts, two-piece brass
with enamel, c. 1989, uniform
wear. Attached to a brown leather
belt. Size 2.75" x 1.5". **Price:** $20
or less.

Greek Scouts, two-piece brass,
c. 1994, uniform wear. Quality of
this buckle nicer than the previous
Greek Scout one. Size 3" x 1.75".
Price: $21 to $40.

Top: Boy Scouts of Nippon
(Japan), two-piece brass, age
unknown, uniform wear. Size
3.25" x 1.75". **Price:** $10 or
less.
Bottom left: Boy Scouts of
Japan, blackened brass friction
buckle, age unknown, uniform
wear. Size 2" x 1.5". **Price:** $10
or less.
Bottom right: Boy Scouts of
Japan, chrome friction buckle,
age unknown, uniform wear. Size
2" x 1.5". **Price:** $10 or less.

Western Style Buckles

Overview

Americans love the Old West to such an extent that a large part of the fun in the newly emerging activity of Cowboy Action Shooting involves dressing for the part, including the buckle. Fortunately for collectors, and Cowboy Action Shooting buffs, the western style buckle is available in hundreds of varieties – old, new, precious metals, rattlesnake skin, etc.

However, not all western style buckles are "created equal." Bigger is better out West. So, the **average** size western buckle probably ranges between 3.75" x 3" and 5" x 3.75".

Size matters: huge, small, and average!
Top: Buckle on steroids, brass and chrome, c. 1992, casual wear. Size 6.5" x 5". **Price:** $61 to $80.
Bottom left: Boy's "Champion" small buckle, chrome, c. 1998, casual wear. Size 2.75" x 2". **Price:** $20 or less.
Bottom right: An average size buckle (still a little large by most non-Western standards), brass and chrome, c. 1990, casual wear. Size 5" x 3.75". **Price:** $41 to $60.

Here are the western style buckles, roughly arranged to first show the traditional type with the characteristic oval shape and rope edge, followed by examples that vary from that description.

Prize buckle, Pampa (Barrel Racing), 2ⁿᵈ Place, brass and chrome, c. 1986, casual wear. Size 3.75" x 3". **Price:** $21 to $40.

Bull roping, brass and chrome, c. 1990, casual wear. Size 5" x 3.75". **Price:** $41 to $60.

Saddle Bronc Riding, brass and chrome, c. 1983, casual wear. Size 5" x 3.75". **Price:** $41 to $60.

A Scorpion? Brass and chrome, c. 2000, casual wear. Size 4.75" x 3.75". **Price:** $41 to $60.

Help Smokey Prevent Forest Fires, brass and chrome with enamel, c. 1994, casual wear. Size 4" x 3". **Price:** $61 to $80.

Louisiana, brass and chrome, c. 1990, casual wear. Size 3.75" x 2.75". **Price:** $21 to $40.

Mexico, silver electroplate on jewelers' bronze with enamel, c. 1998, casual wear. This is an extremely finely crafted buckle. Size 5" x 4". **Price:** $81 to $100.

Running Strong for American Indian Youth, brass, c. 1996, casual wear. Produced by Christian Relief Services. Size 3.5" x 2.5". **Price:** $20 or less.

Filigree Style, brass and enamel, c. 1964, casual wear. Size 3.75" x 2.75". **Price:** $20 or less.

Rattlesnake Skin, over a metal frame with rawhide stitching, c. 1985, casual wear. Size 4.25" x 3". **Price:** $41 to $60.

The Chicken Ranch, La Grange, Texas, brass, c. 1994, casual wear. This is a buckle from a legalized prostitution "facility." Size 3.75" x 2.75". **Price:** $41 to $60.

Boy's "Champion" buckle, chrome, c. 1998, casual wear. Size 2.75" x 2". **Price:** $20 or less.

The State of Texas, brass, c. 1991, casual wear. Size 3.75" x 2.75". **Price:** $20 or less.

Round'em Up, pewter, c. 1994, casual wear. A gift from Sheplers Western Wear Company to its customers. Size 3.75" x 2.75". **Price:** $10 or less.

Hank Williams Photo Buckle, brass with leather and celluloid, c. 1989, casual wear. Size 3.25" x 2.25". **Price:** $20 or less.

121

The Great American Rodeo, matte-finished sterling silver with 24kt. gold electroplate, c. 1988, casual wear. Size 3.5" x 2.5". **Price:** $80 to $100.

Longhorn, brass, c. 1968, casual wear. Also seen in chrome. Size 3.25" x 2". **Price:** $10 or less.

End of the Trail, pewter, c. 1988, casual wear. Size 3.25" x 2.5". **Price:** $20 or less.

Skull in War Bonnet, brass and enamel, age unknown, casual wear. Size 2" x 2.25". **Price:** $20 or less.

Good Luck, brass and chrome, c. 2000, casual wear. Size 2.25" x 1.75". **Price:** $21 to $40.

Top: Miniature chrome buckle on leather bracelet, c. 1999, casual wear. Size 1" x .75". **Price:** $20 or less.
Bottom: Good luck buckle, brass and chrome, c. 2000, casual wear. Size 2.25" x 1.75". **Price:** $21 to $40.

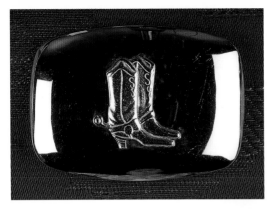

Boots and Spurs, brass and chrome, c. 1989, casual wear. Size 3.75" x 2.5". **Price:** $20 or less.

Lazy Ass Ranch (Leonard, Texas), brass, c. 1999, casual wear. Size 3.75" x 2.75". **Price:** $21 to $40

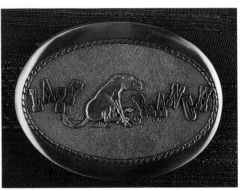

Range Rider, brass, c. 1996, casual wear. Size 3" x 2". **Price:** $20 or less.

Native American Design, sterling silver, c 1999, casual wear. Size 2.25" x 1.75". **Price:** $41 to $60.

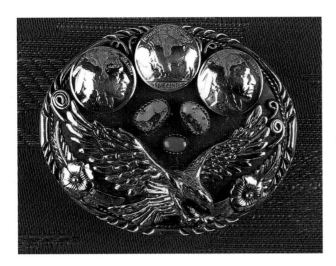

Eagle Plus 15 Cents, chrome with three 5 cent coins, red stone, and turquoise, c. 2000, casual wear. Size 3.25" x 2.75". **Price:** $41 to $60.

Pueblo, chrome with turquoise, c. 1987, casual wear. Size 3" x 2". **Price:** $21 to $40.

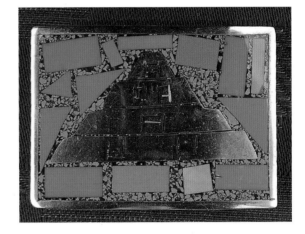

Southwestern, sterling silver with red stone and turquoise, c. 1997, casual wear. Size 3" x 2.25". **Price:** $61 to $80.

Multi-function Buckles

Overview

In the Introduction, the buckle was defined simply as a clasp for a belt. But, over the years, countless imaginative (and in a few cases, wacky) buckle designers have realized the potential carrying capacity of the buckle. Thus, there are buckles that carry (or hold) cigarette lighters, coins, knives, and even guns.

Freedom Arms .22 cal. Black Powder Pistol Buckle, brass buckle, c. 1982, casual wear. Stainless steel pistol with black grips. Pistol released by pressing chrome button behind trigger. Buckle size 4.5" x 2.75". **Price:** $181 to $200.

Complete Freedom Arms Black Powder Pistol Buckle Kit.
Top: Brass buckle showing recess for gun and release button.
Middle: Pistol, stainless steel with black grip panels, and unfluted cylinder.
Bottom: Bullet setting tool, with bullets to the right. Not shown, but included in the set, is a zippered pistol storage rug.

Freedom Arms .22 L.R. Pistol Buckle, brass buckle, c. 1982, casual wear. Matte-finished stainless steel pistol with black grips. Pistol removed by pressing chrome button behind trigger. The buckle is of a different design than that sold with the black powder pistol. Buckle size 4.5" x 2.75". **Price:** $181 to $200.

Freedom Arms Buckle and .22 L.R. Pistol.
Top: Brass buckle showing recess for gun and release button.
Bottom: Pistol, matte-finished stainless steel with black grip panels, and fluted cylinder.

Freedom Arms .22 Mag. Pistol Buckle.
Top: Brass buckle showing recess for gun and release button.
Bottom: Pistol, bright-finished stainless steel with black grip panels, and fluted cylinder. Buckle with pistol size dimensions and price same as Freedom Arms .22 L.R. Pistol Buckle.

North American Arms .22 L.R. Pistol Buckle, pewter buckle, c. 1992, casual wear. Stainless steel pistol with wood grips. Pistol removed by pulling down on retaining clip located behind trigger. Buckle size 5.25" x 3". **Price:** $201 to $220.

North American Arms Buckle and Pistol.
Top: Pewter buckle showing recess for gun and retaining clip. Buckle is sold separately. **Price:** $30.
Bottom: Pistol, bright-finish stainless steel with wood grip panels.

Front View of Sheathed Collins Brothers Belt Buckle Knife, stainless steel buckle knife, leather belt with sheath on back, c. 1988, casual wear. Notice small stud in center of leather buckle, which holds buckle to the belt. Size of buckle portion 1.5" x 2". **Price:** $61 to $80.

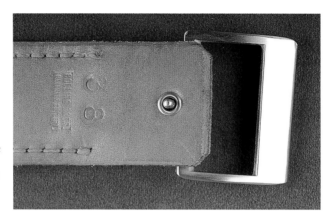

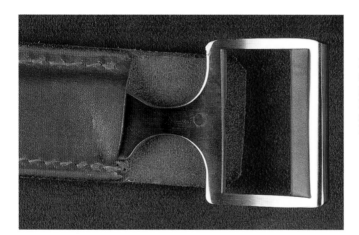

Back View of Sheathed Collins Brothers Belt Buckle Knife, showing sewn leather sheath.

Collins Brothers Buckle Knife and Belt.
Top: Stainless steel knife buckle, high-quality construction, total length 5.5" x 2".
Bottom: Leather belt with eyelet opening (on the right) for stud.

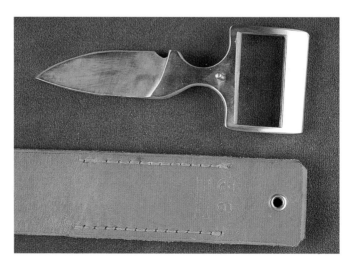

Front View of Sheathed Imported Belt Buckle Knife, black nylon buckle, c. 1988, casual wear. At far right of buckle is a small steel bar. This is a portion of the knife handle. Size of buckle portion 3.5" x 2". **Price:** $20 or less.

Imported Buckle and Knife.
Left: Black nylon buckle, which is the sheath for the knife.
Bottom: Stainless steel knife buckle, total length of knife is 2.75" x 1.75".

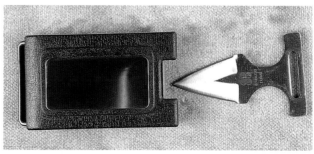

Gerber Legendary Blades Touche® Belt Buckle Knife, wood and fiberglass buckle, c. 1986, casual wear. The diagonal stainless steel bar is, in fact, the knife handle. Size of buckle portion 2.75" x 1.75". **Price:** $41 to $60

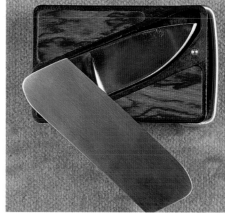

Right: Gerber Legendary Blades Touche® Belt Buckle Knife, with knife handle approximately half way through the clockwise rotation necessary to release it from the buckle.

Gerber Legendary Blades Touche® Belt Buckle Knife, with buckle (top) showing pivot stud in its lower left corner. Knife (bottom) total length is 5". Blade length is 2".

Before wearing any buckle that holds a weapon, please check your state and local laws. And, remember that the guns and knives shown are real weapons — exercise care with them.

Here are some other multi-function buckles.

Lone Star® Beer Bottle Opener Buckle, brass, c. 1998, casual wear. Bottle opener is in the center of the buckle. Size 3.75" x 2.75". **Price:** $21 to $40. P.S.- Opener works with other beer brands, too!

Coin Holder, chrome, c. 1979, casual wear. U.S. dollar-size coin is held in place by a retaining clip on the back of the buckle. Size 3.5" x 2". **Price:** $20 or less.

Lighter Holder, pewter, c. 1997, casual wear. Lighter is held in a "cradle" located at the bottom of the buckle. Caution: this buckle may scratch the lighter. Size 3.5" x 2.75". **Price:** $20 or less.

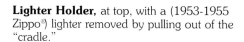

Lighter Holder, at top, with a (1953-1955 Zippo®) lighter removed by pulling out of the "cradle."

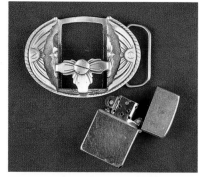

131

Lighter Holder, pewter with enamel, c. 1994, casual wear. Size 3.5" x 2.75". **Price:** $21 to $40.

Lighter Holder, with the lighter removed to show the retaining method. The circular magnet in the center of the recessed area holds any metal Zippo®-style lighter.

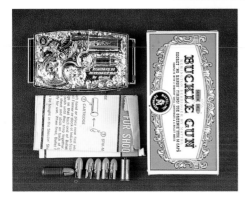

Buckle Gun (Toy) Set, painted chrome over base metal, c. 1959, casual wear. Toy Remington derringer pistol, made by Mattel, spring-mounted to pivot out from the buckle. This mint condition set includes the buckle gun (top), instruction sheet (middle), and several "bullets" and "shells." Original box is to the right. Buckle size 4" x 2.25". **Price:** $61 to $80.

Close-up of Mattel Buckle Gun, showing "safety" at bottom right of buckle (just beneath the words "by Mattel"). After "safety" is moved to deactivate it, the buckle can pivot and "fire" by merely pushing outward with your stomach. Used special "greenie stick-m-caps." The *essential* early 1960s "Cowboys and Indians" toy!

Future Collecting Categories

Overview

The previous chapters illustrated buckles that are already highly collectible: public safety, military, Scouting, western style, and multi-function buckles. No doubt in the future these buckle categories will continue to be avidly collected. But, there are other possibilities.

This chapter takes a look at what surely will become some of the future specialized collecting interest areas. Action buckles, miniatures, animals, clubs and associations, sports, transportation, etc. – all represent areas that you may want to "mark out" for a closer look. In some cases, the existing variety within a category is so small that collecting would be no challenge. But, look for them to proliferate in the future. Oh, and remember what's known in my family as the "Saitta Collecting Rule" – If you have *one* of something, it's a mere curiosity. *Two* of something is a coincidence. But, if you've got *three*, you've started another collection.

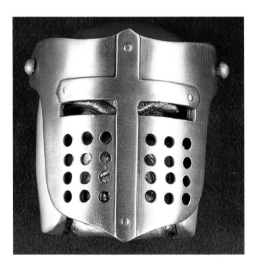

Knight with Visor Down, pewter, c. 1997, casual wear. Size 2" x 2.5". **Price:** $20 or less.

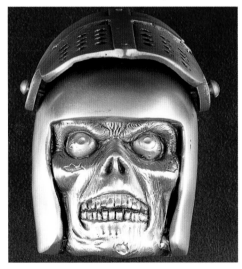

Knight with Visor Up, showing three-dimensional face of skull. Quite detailed.

Four Miniature Buckles, plastic with leather belts, c. 2000, for use with child's action figures, such as G.I. Joe®. Size each .75 x .50. **Price each:** $5.
1. U.S. Army officer, Civil War
2. U.S. Army, enlisted, Civil War
3. German Air Force, World War II
4. Confederate Army, enlisted, Civil War.

Top: Marlboro® Cigarettes, brass, c. 1984, casual wear. Size 3.5" x 2.25".
Price: $10 or less.
Bottom: Big Red® Chewing Tobacco, c. 1997, casual wear. Size 2.75" x 2".
Price: $10 or less.

Raleigh Lights®, brass, c. 1987, casual wear. Size 3.25" x 2.25".
Price: $1.50. (Now, that's a great price!)

Top: Large Budweiser® buckle, pewter and enamel, c. 1998, casual wear. Size 3.25" x 2.25". Serial number on back: 2241. **Price:** $10 or less.
Bottom: Small Budweiser® buckle, pewter and enamel, c. 1998, casual wear. Size 2.25" x 1.75". Serial number on back: 2241A. (Consecutively serial numbered buckles. What will they think of next?) **Price:** $10 or less.

Coors®Beer, brass, c. 1996, casual wear. Size 3" x 2". **Price:** $10 or less.

Lite®, A Fine Pilsner Beer, brass with epoxy, c. 1980, casual wear. Size 3.5" x 2.5". **Price:** $10 or less.

Bear Paw, aluminum, c. 1992, casual wear. Size 3" x 2.5". Made in an adult education industrial arts class at Park View High School, Sterling, Virginia. **Price:** Priceless!

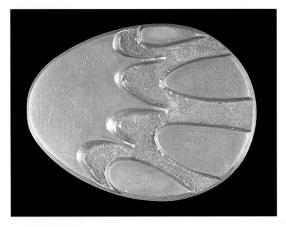

Florida Alligator, brass, c. 1990, casual wear. Size 3.25" x 2.5". **Price:** $20 or less.

Left: A dental hygienist's nightmare. Shark's head pewter buckle, c. 1991, casual wear. Size 2.5" x 2.5". **Price:** $10 or less.
Right: Killer shark, brass, c. 1994, casual wear. Size 3.25" x 2". **Price:** $20 or less.

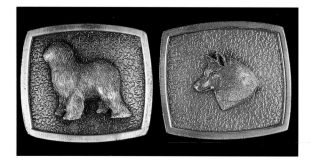

Two Dogs, pewter, c. 1975, casual wear. Size each 2.5" x 2.5". **Price each:** $10 or less.

Eagle Gone Fishing, brass with epoxy, c. 1997, casual wear. Size 4" x 3.75". The landscape features (trees, etc.) are actually feathers embedded in the epoxy. **Price:** $21 to $40.

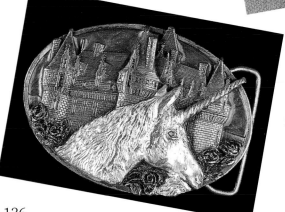

Unicorn and Castle, pewter with epoxy, c. 1983, casual wear. Size 3.5" x 2.75". **Price:** $20 or less.

Strength thru Spinach, U.S. Spinach Growers Assn., Crystal City, Texas, brass over base metal, c. 1989, casual wear. Size 3" in diameter. **Price:** $21 to $40.

Oil Field Trash, pewter with epoxy, c. 1981, casual wear. Size 3.25" x 2.25". **Price:** $21 to $40.

German Chimneysweep, brass box buckle of traditional design, c. 1991, casual wear. Size 2.5" x 1.75". The motto translates to "All for one, one for all." Sounds familiar. Perhaps the Three Musketeers moonlighted. **Price:** $20 or less.

Service Master, brass, c. 1998, casual wear. Size 3" x 1.75". Awarded to certified Buick® service technicians. **Price:** $20 or less.

Back of Service Master Buckle, showing wire stand. Buckle can be worn or displayed.

Coca-Cola® Employee Buckle, chrome over base metal with a color celluloid center, age unknown, uniform wear. Size 2.25" x 1.25". Worn on a red nylon belt. **Price:** $21 to $40.

Coca-Cola® Company, "Feel on Top of the World," brass, casual wear. Size 2.75" x 4". The author purchased this buckle in 1971, probably around the time of its manufacture. The back of the buckle, however, has an inscription alleging that the buckle was produced for the "Trans-Pan Exposition, San Francisco, 1915." **Price:** $21 to $40.

Missouri School of Mines, University of Missouri, Rolla, brass, c. 1987, casual wear. Size 3.25" x 2.25". **Price:** $20 or less.

Top: New Mexico School of Mines, bronze, c. 1999, casual wear. Size 3" x 1.5". There's a story to this buckle. For now, thanks to Deanna, Sarah, Chris and Tim. **Price:** $21 to $40.
Bottom: New Mexico Bureau of Mine Inspection, bronze, c. 1994, casual wear. Size 2.25" x 1.25". **Price:** $20 or less.

McDonald's® Employee, brass over base metal (with much of the plating worn off), friction style buckle, c. 1977, uniform wear. Size 2" x 1.5". **Price:** $21 to $40.

Electrician, brass, c. 1980, casual wear. Size 3.25" x 2.5". **Price:** $20 or less.

Colt® (Firearms), Past, Present, Future, 24kt. gold electroplate over chrome, c. 1998, casual wear. Size 4" x 3.5". **Price:** $81 to $100.

Old Reliable (Ammunition Company), brass Anson Mills reproduction, c. 1988, unknown wear. Size 3" x 3". **Price:** $20 or less.

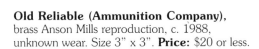

Pacific AgriLands, Inc., brass, c. 1998, casual wear. Size 3.5" x 2.25". **Price:** $20 or less.

Top: Telephone Pioneering Together, Telephone Pioneers of America, pewter, c. 1984, casual wear. Size 3" x 2.25". **Price:** $21 to $40.
Bottom: Bell® Telephone Logo, brass, age unknown, casual wear. Size 2.5" in diameter. **Price:** $20 or less.

Top: Pool Well Servicing, brass, age unknown, casual wear. Size 3.75" x 2.75". **Price:** $20 or less.
Bottom: Iveco (Trucks of North America, Inc.), c. 1984, casual wear. Size 2.75" x 1.75". **Price:** $20 or less.

St. John's No. 20 (Knights Templar), chrome with enamel, age unknown, uniform wear. Size 2.5" x 3". The Knights Templar (KT), Grand Encampment of the United States, has an estimated 300,000 members. **Price:** $41 to $60.

Highlands Commandery No. 30 (Knights Templar), chrome with enamel, age unknown, uniform wear. Size 2.25" x 2.75". **Price:** $41 to $60.

Yonkers Commandery, 47 KT, chrome with enamel, age unknown, uniform wear. Size 2.75" x 2". The Knights Templar was founded in 1816. **Price:** $21 to $40.

Left: Bethany Commandery, 83 KT, brass, age unknown, casual wear. Size 2.25" x 2.5". **Price:** $21 to $40. **Right:** Battle Creek No. 33 (Knights Templar), chrome with enamel (some of which is chipped), age unknown, casual wear. Size 2.25" x 2.75". **Price:** $21 to $40.

Top: Masonic symbols, bronze with enamel, c. 1978, casual wear. Size 3" x 2". Worldwide the "Craft" has millions of members. **Price:** $21 to $40.
Bottom: Masonic emblem, silver electroplate with brass and enamel, c. 1946, casual wear. Size 1.75" x 1". **Price:** $20 or less.

Left: Shriners, Hadji, bronze, c. 1986, casual wear. Size 3" x 2". The complete name of the organization is the "Imperial Council of the Ancient Arabic Order of the Mystic Shrine." **Price:** $20 or less.
Right: Shriners symbol, pewter with bronze, age unknown, casual wear. Size 3" x 2.25". **Price:** $20 or less.

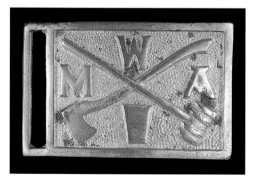

Modern Woodmen of America, brass with some light corrosion, age unknown, uniform wear. Size 3" x 2". Originally attached to a white cotton belt. There are close to a million members of this organization. **Price:** $20 or less.

North American Hunting Club, Life Member, gold and rhodium electroplate over brass, c. 1994, casual wear. Size 3.25" x 2.5". **Price:** $41 to $60.

NRA (National Rifle Association) Leadership Award, pewter, c. 1983, casual wear. Size 3.5" x 2.25". **Price:** $20 or less.

Inkatha Freedom Party (Republic of South Africa), brass, c. 1988, casual wear. Attached to a brown leather belt. Size 3.5" x 3.25". **Price:** $21 to $40.

Do It in a Van, pewter, c. 1976, casual wear. Size 3" x 2.25". **Price:** $20 or less.

Four Feet, pewter, c. 1985, casual wear. Size 4.25" x 3". **Price:** $20 or less.

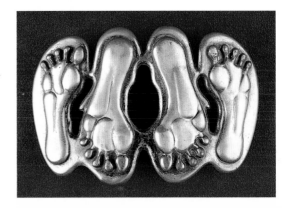

Lounging Lady, pewter, c. 1979, casual wear. Size 4.25" x 1.5". **Price:** $20 or less.

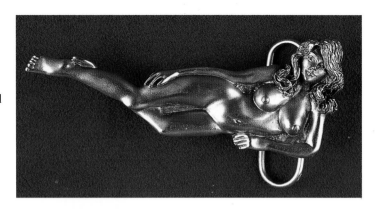

Man in the Moon with Guest, pewter, c. 1979, casual wear. Size 3.25" in diameter. **Price:** $20 or less.

Male Chauvinist, brass, c. 1973, casual wear. Size 2.25" in diameter. **Price:** $21 to $40.

Marijuana Leaf, brass, c. 1969, casual wear. Size 3.25" x 2.5". **Price:** $41 to $60.

Marrakech Express (Store), Leesburg, Virginia, brass with leather center, c. 1977, casual wear. Size 3" x 2.5". **Price:** $21 to $40.

I'd Walk a Mile for an Acapulco Gold, Available Everywhere, brass, c. 1976, casual wear. Size 3.75" x 2.25". **Price:** $21 to $40.

Guns N Roses, brass, c. 1993, casual wear. Size 3" x 2.25". **Price:** $20 or less.

Hard Rock Cafe, Save the Planet, pewter friction buckle, c. 1976, unknown wear. Size 2" x 1.5". **Price:** $10 or less.

Left: Bowling Award, C.P.O. (Chief Petty Officers') Club, GTMO Bay, Cuba, brass, c. 1948, casual wear. Size 2" x 2". **Price:** $21 to $40.
Right: Most Improved Average, League Award, American Bowling Congress, brass, c. 1968-1969, casual wear. Size 2" x 1". **Price:** $20 or less.

Left: 13th Olympic Winter Games, Lake Placid, brass, c. 1980, casual wear. Size 3.75" x 2.25". **Price:** $21 to $40.
Right: Lake Placid, Winter Olympics, brass, c. 1980, casual wear. Size 2.75" in diameter. **Price:** $21 to $40.

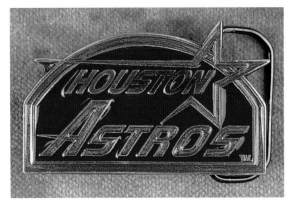

Houston Astros™, pewter with epoxy, c. 1994, casual wear. Size 3" x 2.75". **Price:** $20 or less.

Texas Rangers Baseball Club™, pewter, c. 1994, casual wear. Size 3" x 2.5". **Price:** $20 or less.

Minnesota Timberwolves™, pewter with epoxy, c. 1994, casual wear. Size 2.75" x 2.25". **Price:** $20 or less.

Soccer, brass, c. 1977, casual wear. Size 3.25" x 2.5". **Price:** $10 or less.

Left: 33rd Anniversary Zebco 33® (Fishing Reels), brass, c. 1988, casual wear. Over 22 million Zebco 33® reels had been sold by 1988. Size 2.75" x 2.25". **Price:** $20 or less.
Right: I'd Rather be Fishing, pewter, c. 1994, casual wear. Size 2.75" x 2". **Price:** $10 or less.

Left: Large Mouth Bass, c. 1979, brass with suede and epoxy, casual wear. Size 2.75" x 2.5". **Price:** $20 or less.
Right: Bass Anglers Sportsman Society, B.A.S.S., pewter, c. 1988, casual wear. Size 3" x 2". **Price:** $20 or less.

Aloha (Surfing), brass, c. 1977, casual wear. Size 3.5" x 2.5". **Price:** $20 or less.

Top: Side view of train, c. 1978, brass, casual wear. Size 3.25" x 2". **Price:** $20 or less.
Bottom: Comin' round the mountain, brass, c. 1975, casual wear. Size 3.25" x 2". **Price:** $20 or less.

149

New Zealand Shipping Company, tentative identification, two-piece brass, c. 1977, uniform wear. Size 3" x 2". **Price:** $21 to $40.

Top: USAir, age unknown, brass over base metal, uniform wear. Size 1.75" x 1.25". **Price:** $20 or less.
Bottom: USAir, brass over base metal, age unknown, uniform wear. Slightly different design than above. Excessive wear reduces value. Size 1.75" x 1.25". **Price:** $10 or less.

Wells Fargo & Co., Since 1852, brass, c. 1975, casual wear. Size 3.5" x 2.25". **Price:** $20 or less.

Top: Henry Ford Automobiles, Record Model T Year, Detroit, brass over base metal, age unknown, casual wear. Size 3" x 2.25". **Price:** $20 or less.
Bottom: Neville Ford Dealership, brass, age unknown, casual wear. Size 2.5" x 1.5". **Price:** $10 or less.

Truck Drivers Move the Nation,
pewter, c. 1987, casual wear. Size 3"
x 2.25". **Price:** $20 or less.

Hot Wheels®, Formula Fever®,
brass, c. 1984, casual wear. Size
2.25" x 1.5". **Price:** $10 or less.

The Highway to Hell,
pewter, c. 1991, casual wear.
Size 3" x 2.25". **Price:** $21 to
$40.

Honda® Motorcycle, chrome
with some wear, c. 1969, casual
wear. Size 3.25" x 2.25". **Price:**
$20 or less.

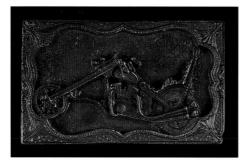

Road Machine, brass, c. 1979, casual wear. Size 3.5" x 2.25". **Price:** $10 or less.

Top: Harley-Davidson Motor-cycles®, chrome, age unknown, casual wear. Size 2.25" x 1.25". **Price:** $20 or less.
Bottom: Harley-Davidson® (in script), chrome, age unknown, casual wear. Size 2.25" x 1.25". **Price:** $10 or less.

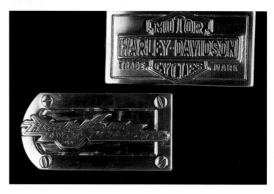

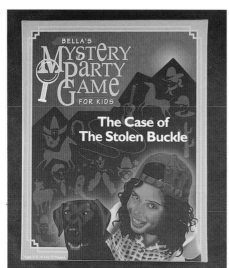

The Case of the Stolen Buckle. Yes, Virginia, there is a belt buckle game. Designed for ages 8 to 14, up to 8 players solve a mystery. **Price:** approximately $20, c. 1999.

Kids, Look What You Get: scorecards, nameplates, instructions, an audio tape, **and** a real belt buckle (right center), pewter, size 2.5" x 2".

Our American Heritage, The Second Amendment, brass, c. 1976, casual wear. Reverse contains the entire transcript of the Second Amendment. Size 4" x 2.25". **Price:** $21 to $40.

The Minutemen, 1776-1976, brass, c. 1976, casual wear. Size 3.25" x 2". **Price:** $20 or less.

Snow Bird, brass, c. 1998, casual wear. Size 3.75" x 2.75". **Price:** $21 to $40.

Mythical Asian Creature, brass, c. 1974, casual wear. Size 2" x 2.5". **Price:** $20 or less.

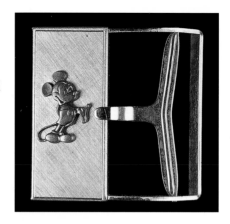

Mickey Mouse®, brass, c. 1973, casual wear. Size 2" x 2". **Price:** $21 to $40.

100 Years of Liberty, brass with gold electroplate, c. 1986, casual wear. Celebrates the 100th anniversary of the completion of the Statue of Liberty. Size 3.25" x 2.5". **Price:** $20 or less.

American Equality, Women's Liberation, Votes for Women, Free Speech, brass, age unknown, casual wear. At the base of the buckle, in extremely fine print, is "Man' f. by U.S. Women' s Liberation Movement HQ. N.Y." Size 4" x 2.25". **Price:** $20 or less.

Crosman Copperhead® **Super Round BBs,** copper over base metal, c. 1997, casual wear. Size 2.75" x 2". **Price:** $10 or less.

American Fisheries Society, brass, age unknown, casual wear. Size 3" x 2". **Price:** $21 to $40.

Al, Egypt, handmade from sheet brass, age unknown, casual wear. Size 3.75" x 2.5". **Price:** $21 to $40.

KKK (Ku Klux Klan), brass with leather and epoxy, age unknown, casual wear. Size 3.25" x 2.25". **Price:** $20 or less.

Mystery Buckles

Well, these are a mystery to me, anyway. If you can provide a positive identification I'd be very appreciative. Here's what little tentative information I have about these eight buckles.

Reportedly from Thailand, chrome, age unknown, Size 2" x 1.5". **Price:** $20 or less.

Reportedly Republic of South Vietnam Navy, gold electroplate over brass, c. 1968, uniform wear. Very fine quality. Back has two initials, FB, stamped into catch. Size 1.5" x 1.75". **Price:** $41 to $60.

No information, two-piece chrome on white cotton belt, age unknown. Size 1.5" x 1.5". **Price:** $10 or less.

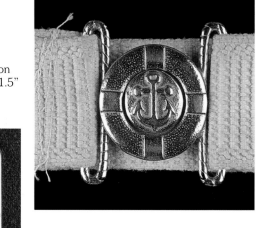

Reportedly Japanese Navy, Enlisted, chrome, W.W.II era, uniform wear. Size 1" x 1.25". **Price:** $21 to $40.

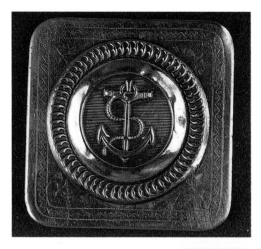

Reportedly U.S. Navy, steel, c. 1890s, unknown wear. Size 2" x 2". **Price if 1890s U.S. Navy:** $61 to $80.

Reportedly both are South American Military.
Left: two-piece chrome, crudely finished. No markings. Size 3" x 2". **Price:** $20 or less. **Right:** two-piece brass, well-made. May be Argentinean Army officer. Size 2.75" x 2". **Price:** $21 to $40.

Regiment Artillery, brass, one-piece construction, age unknown. Size 1" x .5". **Price:** $10 or less.

Compass Rose, two-piece brass over base metal, c. 1950s, unknown wear. Size 2.5" x 1.25". **Price:** $10 or less.

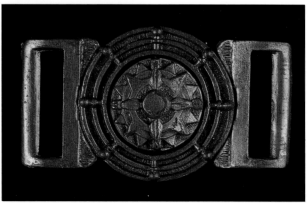

Resources

Although buckle collecting as an *organized* hobby is virtually non-existent, there are still resources available to you. This chapter reviews two such resources: publications and Internet sites.

There are several publications that are essential if you collect military buckles. German military buckle collectors should have these books available:

Reid, Thomas. *German Belt Buckles*. Mt. Ida, Arkansas: Lancer Militaria, 1989.

This classic reference book covers in detail the period from the mid-1800s to the end of World War II. If you intend to collect German military buckles of this period, this book is a "must have." It includes the history of the development of the German military buckle, information on manufacturing, trademark and product codes, a bibliography and glossary, plus many, many clearly illustrated buckles.

Evans, Bob. *Third Reich Belt Buckles: An Illustrated Handbook and Price Guide*. Atglen, Pennsylvania: Schiffer Publishing Ltd., 1999.

This book is another necessity for German military buckle collectors. Its focus is on only those World War II German military buckles that depict a swastika (with one exception). There are over 125 full-color buckle photographs that feature both the front and the back of each buckle plus information about hallmarks and pricing.

Lumsden, Robin. *Detecting the Fakes: A Collector's Guide to Third Reich Militaria*. New York: Hippocrene Books, Inc., 1989.

Third Reich buckles have been reproduced extensively, often with no other purpose than to deceive the unwary. Although this book's section on buckles is only four pages in length, it serves as a very handy reminder of the indicators of genuine versus fake World War II German buckles.

If you collect American military buckles here are some further useful texts:

O'Donnell, Michael J. and J. Duncan Campbell. *American Military Belt Plates*. Alexandria, Virginia: O'Donnell Publications, 1996.

Since the classic Sidney Kerksis' book, *Plates and Buckles of the American Military, 1795-1874*, is hard to get, this has emerged as the essential American military buckle collector's book. In 616 pages it describes hundreds of buckles from the Revolutionary War to the early 1900s. The 1026 buckles are depicted in black and white photographs, front and back, along with explanatory text.

Mullinax, Steve E. *Confederate Belt Buckles and Plates.* Alexandria, Virginia: O'Donnell Publications, 1991.

This book does for the Southern buckles what the previous book did for the other American Civil War buckles. There is some overlap between the two books in that both cover militia buckles and plates of the Southern states. However, each book goes far beyond that into other areas. The Mullinax text provides black and white photographs, front and back, of 454 buckles and plates.

If you collect North Vietnamese and Viet Cong buckles, you should have this book available:

Emering, Edward J. *Weapons and Field Gear of the North Vietnamese Army and Viet Cong.* Atglen, Pennsylvania: Schiffer Publishing Ltd., 1998.

Only one page in this book addresses buckles. However, the color photographs of the eight buckles are of high quality and should prove helpful in authenticating these military items.

Within the covert action community, there has always been interest in small, concealable tools. The belt buckle, because of its utility, is often an ideal location for hidden weapons and other such clandestine accoutrements. Here are several books that include at least a few descriptions of such buckles:

Minnery, John. *CIA Catalog of Clandestine Weapons, Tools, and Gadgets.* Boulder, Colorado: Paladin Press, 1990.

Find out about buckles that conceal saws and compasses. The book also describes the 22-karat gold buckle issued to CIA agents in Vietnam to use as a source of emergency funds.

Gawkowski, Glenn D. *The GDG Reports: Exotic and Covert Weapons.* Boulder, Colorado: Paladin Press, 1988.

Of the 57 weapons described, four of them are contained in buckles.

Melton, H. Keith. *The Ultimate Spy Book.* New York: DK Publishing, Inc., 1996.

There are only two concealment buckles featured in this book: a microphone buckle and a belt buckle pistol. But, if you have any interest in the intelligence field, this book provides a broad photographic overview of the entire arena.

Finally, here are a few internet sites and commercial sources that will help you with your buckle collecting:

Ricardo Hernandez Canto, who lives in Mexico, has the information you need on Boy Scout buckles. He is not a dealer, but a highly informed and very helpful collector. And, he's an honest person to trade with. His web site is devoted to the display of Scout buckles from around the world. It is www.geocities.com/Pipeline/5983/BUCKLES.HTML

Hanover Brass Foundry, 5155 Cold Harbor Rd., Mechanicsville, Virginia 23111. Gary Williams has been casting buckles for 30 years. His high quality reproduction Civil War buckles are used by reenactors who value authenticity. You can check his web site — www.hanoverbrass.com — for current models. If you are having difficulty determining if a Civil War buckle is the real thing or one of Gary's reproductions, he will help you out.

Lazy Ass Ranch, 19051 FM 981, Leonard, Texas 75452. Rex Hogue has an extensive selection of western style buckles, including his special "Lazy Ass Ranch" model. His web site is: www.lazyassranch.com

The Buckleman, P.O. Box 30, Brooklyn, New York 11204, operates an on-line buckle store. He's got those cool action buckles, plus a lot more. His web site is: www.thebuckleman.com

TBW Industries, 59 Victory Lane, Los Gatos, California 95031. If your agency or organization is in the market for a well-designed buckle, then try TBW. They've got over 20 years experience casting buckles, and are especially well known for their work with law enforcement and fire agencies. The web site is www.tbwindustries.com

There are many other excellent buckle resources—both for research information and for suppliers. And, with a bit of checking, you should be able to turn up some *local* resources in your own community.

If you've got information about other resources please contact me (Saitta@aol.com) so that I may add them to future editions of this book. Thanks, and good collecting.